G000150034

A guide to
The South Devon and Dorset
Coast Paths

Also by Roland Gant

Listen, confides the wind
How like a wilderness
Me'sentente cordiale (with Nadia Legrand)
Five of a kind
World in a jug
The prose of Edward Thomas
The countryside of Edward Thomas
Dorset villages
Stubble burning

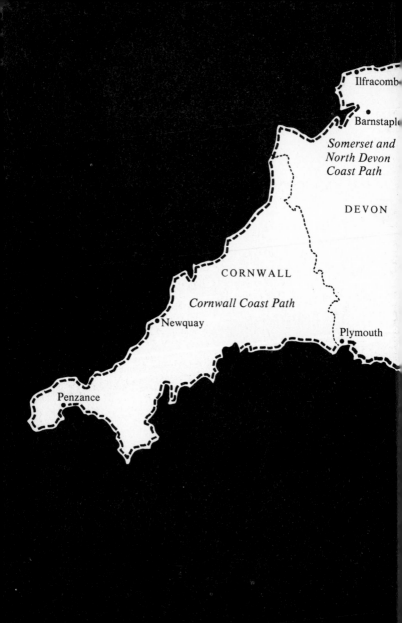

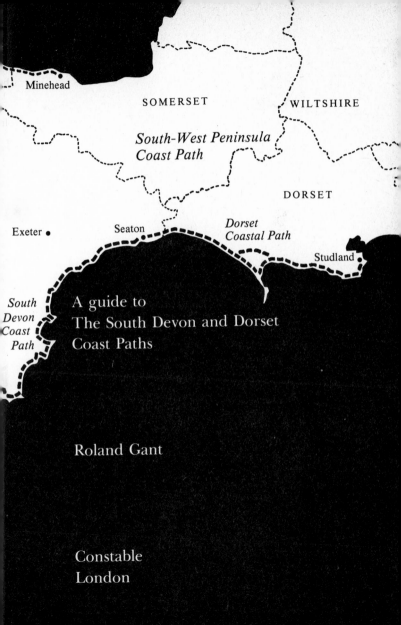

Minehead

SOMERSET   WILTSHIRE

*South-West Peninsula
Coast Path*

DORSET

Exeter •   Seaton   *Dorset
Coastal Path*

Studland

*South
Devon
Coast
Path*

A guide to
The South Devon and Dorset
Coast Paths

Roland Gant

Constable
London

First published in Great Britain 1982
by Constable and Company Limited
10 Orange Street London WC2H 7EG
Copyright © 1982 by Roland Gant
ISBN 0 09 462440 2
Set in 9pt Baskerville by
Inforum Ltd, Portsmouth
Printed in Great Britain by
Ebenezer Baylis & Son Ltd
The Trinity Press, Worcester
and London

Contents

Illustrations		7
Acknowledgements		9
Maps		10
Metric conversion table		11
Country Code		12
Introduction		13

THE SOUTH DEVON COAST PATH

1	Plymouth	29
2	Plymouth to the River Yealm	30
3	The Yealm to the Erme	35
4	The Erme to the Avon	41
5	The Avon to Salcombe	44
6	Salcombe	50
7	Salcombe to Prawle Point	53
8	Prawle Point to Start Point	56
9	Start Point to Dartmouth	58
10	Dartmouth	69
11	Dartmouth to Brixham	71
12	Brixham to the Teign	74
13	The Teign to the Exe	78
14	The Exe to the Otter	80
15	The Otter to the Sid	88
16	Sidmouth to Seaton	92
17	Seaton to Lyme Regis	104

THE DORSET COAST PATH

| 1 | Lyme Regis | 117 |
| 2 | Lyme Regis to West Bay | 120 |

3	West Bay and Bridport	127
4	West Bay to Abbotsbury	130
5	Abbotsbury	136
6	Abbotsbury to Weymouth	139
7	Weymouth	143
8	Weymouth to Lulworth Cove	151
9	Lulworth Cove to Kimmeridge	162
10	Kimmeridge to Swanage	173
11	Swanage	185
12	Swanage to Studland and South Haven Point	187

ALTERNATIVE HIGH-LEVEL INLAND ROUTE
West Bexington to Osmington Mills

	Introduction	197
1	West Bexington to the Hardy Monument	198
2	Hardy Monument to Bincombe	201
3	Bincombe to Osmington Mills	207

WALKING ON THE CHESIL BEACH

Introduction	217
The Chesil Beach: Abbotsbury to Ferry Bridge (Weymouth)	218
Appendix: Useful information and addresses	222
Selected Bibliography	230
Index	233

Illustrations

The South Devon Coast Path

Map of the route	18–27
Going down to Wembury	32
Newton Ferrers	34
Yealm Mouth, from the Newton Ferrers side	36
Yealm Mouth, from the Noss Mayo side	36
Looking east along the Coast Path from Revelstoke	38
The top of Beacon Hill, looking east towards St Anchorite's Rock	41
The salmon fishermen's hut at Bantham	45
The 'pierced stone' at Thurlestone	46
Hope Cove	47
Kingsbridge Estuary, looking inland	49
Sharpitor House and gardens, Salcombe	52
A lookout tower on the way to the Gara Rock Hotel	55
Castle Ferry, Dartmouth	67
The Dart Estuary	68
Dartmouth Castle	70
The Coast Path rounds Sharkham Point	73
Steam rules between Dartmouth and Torbay	75
Oddicombe funicular	77
'Osokoze' at Exmouth	81
A friend at Sandy Bay	82
Hayes Barton near Budleigh Salterton	85
South Farm, close to the point where the Otter is crossed	87
East Bank of the Otter Estuary	89
Looking east down to Sidmouth	90
Church Living, Branscombe	98
Great Seaside Farm, Branscombe	101
Beer	102
The tramway at Seaton	103
The Coast Path above Axmouth: looking over Seaton Bay to Beer Head	106

The Dorset Coast Path

Map of the route   110–116
Looking down on Lyme Regis, where the two Coast Paths meet   118
Colmer's Hill, just west of Bridport   127
Looking east, through Abbotsbury   137
The Great Tithe Barn, Abbotsbury   138
Nothe Fort and Gardens, Weymouth   147
Weymouth Harbour   149
The site of Ringstead medieval village   154
St Catherine's by the Sea, Holworth   156
Mintrice – a Coast Path companion   157
Coast Guard Cottages on White Nothe   158
The view eastwards from White Nothe   158
Is this how Scratchy Bottom got its name?   160
Swyre Head and Durdle Door   160
Durdle Door, with St Oswald's Bay beyond   161
The path up Hambury Tout from Lulworth Cove   161
Stair Hole, Lulworth   163
The Fossil Forest: tufa at Lulworth   166
The church of St Mary at Lulworth Castle   168
Lulworth Castle   168
Ruins at Tyneham village   172
Oil well 'nodding donkey' pump, Kimmeridge Bay   174
Clavel Tower, Kimmeridge   176
Corfe Castle   178
St Aldhelm's Chapel, St Aldhem's Head   180
The Great Globe, Swanage   184
Durlston Castle, now a cafeteria   184
The church of St Nicholas, Studland   190
Gargoyles at St Nicholas   190
Shell Bay, Dorset: at the end (or beginning) of the Coast Path   193
Going down to Bincombe village   206
Spring Bottom, Preston   208
Track from the White Horse Hill down to Osmington village   210
King George III, White Horse Hill   210
The forge at Osmington   212
Looking westwards along the Chesil Beach   219

Acknowledgements

I should like to thank all those kindly strangers between Plymouth and Poole who pointed me in the right direction, told me of short cuts, warned me of hazards, offered food, drink, local history, and helped me on my way.

In particular I wish to thank Philip Carter, Secretary of the South West Way Association, for his valuable advice and comments on reading a very rough draft of this book, and the Membership Secretaries of the Association, first Mrs D. Y. Lancey and later Mrs M. Macleod.

I am grateful to Rodney Legg, writer and founder/editor of *Dorset, the County Magazine*, for identifying photographs and for proof-reading, and to Diana and Romilly Whitehead for lending me their house in Salcombe. Sometimes I had company along the way. Thank you Nadia, Alasdair and Mintrice.

R.G
Armswell, Dorset
September 1982

Maps

South Devon Coast Path
1:100 000	Bartholomew National Map Series 2 South Devon
1:50 000	Ordnance Survey Sheets 192, 193, 201, 202
1:25 000	Ordnance Survey Sheets SX 45, 54, 64, 63/73/83, 74/84, 85/95, 86/96, 87/97, SY 08/18, 29/39
1:25 000	Ordnance Survey Outdoor Leisure Map South Devon

Dorset Coast Path
1:100 000	Bartholomew National Map Series 4 Dorset
1:50 000	Ordnance Survey Sheets 193, 194, 195
1:25 000	Ordnance Survey Sheets SY 29/39, 49/59, 58, 67/77, 68/78, 87/97, SZ 07, 88/98, SZ 08
1:25 000	Ordnance Survey Outdoor Leisure Map Purbeck

Metric Conversion Tables

The bold figures in the central columns can be read as either the metric or the British measure. Thus 1 inch = 25.4 millimetres; or 1 millimetre = 0.039 inches

Inches		Millimetres
0.039	1	25.4
0.079	2	50.8
0.118	3	76.2
0.157	4	101.6
0.197	5	127.0
0.236	6	152.4
0.276	7	177.8
0.315	8	203.2
0.354	9	228.6

Feet		Metres
3.281	1	0.305
6.562	2	0.610
9.843	3	0.914
13.123	4	1.219
16.404	5	1.524
19.685	6	1.829
22.966	7	2.134
26.247	8	2.438
29.528	9	2.743

Yards		Metres
1.094	1	0.914
2.187	2	1.829
3.281	3	2.743
4.374	4	3.658
5.468	5	4.572

Cu feet		Cu Metres
35.315	1	0.028
70.629	2	0.057
105.944	3	0.085
141.259	4	0.113
176.573	5	0.142
211.888	6	0.170
247.203	7	0.198
282.517	8	0.227
317.832	9	0.255

Miles		Kilometres
0.621	1	1.609
1.243	2	3.219
1.864	3	4.828
2.486	4	6.437
3.107	5	8.047
3.728	6	9.656
4.350	7	11.265
4.971	8	12.875
5.592	9	14.484

Sq feet		Sq metres
10.764	1	0.093
21.528	2	0.186
32.292	3	0.297
43.056	4	0.372
53.820	5	0.465
64.583	6	0.557
75.347	7	0.650
86.111	8	0.753
96.875	9	0.836

Sq yards		Sq metres
1.196	1	0.836
2.392	2	1.675
3.588	3	2.508
4.784	4	3.345
5.980	5	4.181

Gallons		Litres
0.220	1	4.546
0.440	2	0.092
0.660	3	13.638
0.880	4	18.184
1.100	5	22.731
1.320	6	27.277
1.540	7	31.823
1.760	8	36.369
1.980	9	40.915

Country Code

1 Guard against all risks of fire
2 Fasten all gates
3 Keep dogs under proper control
4 Keep to paths across farmland
5 Avoid damaging fences, hedges and walls
6 Leave no litter
7 Safeguard water supplies
8 Protect wild life, wild pland snd trees
9 Go carefully on country roads
10 Respect to life of the countryside

Introduction

From Minehead in Somerset and around the South West
Peninsula of England runs the longest of the official
long-distance footpaths, ending at South Haven Point in Dorset, a
short ferry and bus ride from Bournemouth. It is usually
described as covering 515 miles but some of those who have
walked along it, and the South West Way Association which was
formed to promote the interests of users of the South West
Peninsula Coast Path, think that it is more, possibly as much as
541 miles. It does not matter what the precise distance is (and it
can never be precise); in fact, the longer it is the better.

It was not an instant creation. Most of the paths had been used
for centuries, until 1913 – by the Coast Guard when it was a
preventive service, by the smugglers whose activities were to be
prevented, and by honest but mostly poor travellers whose work
or inclinations drew them through the towns and villages of the
Channel coast. At times when England feared invasion from
Europe – by the Spanish in the sixteenth century, by the French
in the eighteenth and nineteenth centuries, and by the Germans
in the twentieth century – watch was kept, forts were built,
beacons stood ready for the torch, and radar ears were pricked.
Now the paths that were trodden by Excisemen, Fencibles and
Home Guards are open to all who walk in peace and for healthful
pleasure.

The concept of long-distance leisure paths passed into law with
the National Parks and Access to the Countryside Act of 1949, as
a result of which the South West Way came into being, mainly by
the linking of existing coastal rights-of-way. It has for
convenience been officially assembled into four geographical
sections.

The Cornish Path (sometimes further designated as
the North Cornwall and the South Cornwall Coast Paths of 137
and 133 miles respectively) was opened on 19 May 1973. The
South Devon and Dorset Coast Paths, of 93 and 72 miles

respectively, were opened together on 14 September 1974. The Somerset and North Devon Coast Path of 82 miles in length was opened on 20 May 1978. To my description of the South Devon and Dorset Coast Paths I have added one officially approved alternative (the High-Level Coast Path between West Bexington and Osmington in Dorset), and an unofficial and personal suggestion (a walk along the Chesil Beach, also in Dorset).

What are the chief characteristics of the South Devon and Dorset section of the South West Peninsula Path? First of all, there is the infinite variety of landscape within comparatively short distances. Within half an hour of climbing a steep path to a clifftop golden with gorse, one can be walking through woods that slope down to a wide estuary, or making a detour to swim in a secluded cove. Sometimes cliffs and offshore stacks are of dark red sandstone; in other places chalk cliffs stretch ahead for miles, making a scalloped frame to the sea. There are curving sandy bays and the massive pebble reef of the Chesil Beach, and some walking close to the sea, where the clifftop wind and thunder of breakers on the rocks are exchanged for the metallic susurration of reeds and the scolding and clicketing gossip of waterfowl. There are fishing villages and mere nicks in the coastline into which fishermen draw their boats and sort their catch, walks along esplanades to get from one end of a typical English seaside town to the other, taking in all that tradition provides – the shelters with slatted seats, ornamental rockeries, pots of tea with scones, cream and strawberry jam, crazy golf, beach huts, amazing railways like the Torbay and Dartmouth Steam Line and the funicular at Oddicombe, which if it is not *art nouveau* is artfully original.

On the Coast Path or just off it are villages of stone and thatch, small towns of Georgian and Regency houses built at the time of the passion for sea-bathing and Jane Austen's inimitable novels about the society that went down to the sea. There are villages whose inhabitants have lived for centuries from the fish they caught, processed, stored, and sold; or from the stone they cut by hand from the downs and cliffs, to be transported overland by pack-horses and carts or loaded into the barges at the foot of the cliffs. Some villages have been destroyed by the sea, and in others boats have been built to battle with the tides. There are towns that have sent ships and sailors against England's enemies – and sometimes against those who were not officially enemies but whose ships laden with merchandise and sometimes treasure were worth intercepting or wrecking. Everywhere the South West Way touches history, from Iron Age forts like Flowers Barrow, the ports of fourteenth-century wine-traders, Elizabethan voyagers, Puritan emigrants, Monmouth's West-Country-based attempt to seize the Crown, the determination to repel Bonaparte, naval bases and colleges, down to the Atomic Energy Establishment at Winfrith in Dorset.

In practical terms, the South Devon and Dorset Coast Paths offer very varied terrain. There is, of course, no mountain walking; and there is neither moor nor marshland to cross, but one comes close to both. Crossing Bolberry Down in Devon or Golden Cap, the highest point on the coast of Southern England, is akin to moorland walking; and Slapton Ley in Devon and Little Sea behind Studland Bay in Dorset are marshy lakes close to the Path. There are some stiff climbs and steep descents, and long and lonely stretches over high downland and through the landslip wilderness on the Devon-Dorset border.

Beginners and all who are willing to try should take on this invigorating route in the company of experienced walkers. There is no pleasure in getting tired, footsore, lost, or just fed up with it all. These are annoyances that can easily be avoided by not trying to cover too great distances in one go, by sticking to the Coast Path and, in the event of straying from it, by retracing the way back to the nearest Coast Path signpost. When either very lost or when the weather becomes too foul to walk with enjoyment, look at the compass and the map and head inland to the nearest village and road.

Even in the height of summer it can be cold or damp (or both) in the evening or suddenly during the day. That prevailing westerly wind and the Atlantic Ocean are never far away. Carry some woollen pullovers, socks, bonnets, and rainproof outerwear, and have the pleasure of cursing the extra weight when the sun beats down again. Anti-sunburn cream, lipsalve against salt winds, elastic bandages against an awkward fall or the unseen pot-hole, Elastoplast for blisters and grazes, torch, matches, whistle, Kendal Mintcake, something warm to climb into and something warm to drink (or the means of making a warm drink) – all this goes without saying. Think of them, carry them, and odds are that they will not be needed. A camera, a monocular (less heavy than fieldglasses), good maps, a compass, and a guide to the Coast Path add to the immediate enjoyment and the record of what is there to see and enjoy. Familiarity with the bus routes close to the Coast Path is important, and suggestions are made in the Bibliography and Appendix. Although the route is neither over a desert nor across a wilderness, there are occasions when a telephone kiosk and a nearby bus become important. I have walked most of the Coast Path several times and in different seasons, and I have always found people who live along or close to the route very helpful with information about local topography, bed-and-breakfast places and pubs, transport, and advice about where to ask for permission to camp for the night. Courteous enquiries by walkers who obviously neither trespass nor scatter litter are generally met by helpful answers.

The South Devon Coast Path

1 **Plymouth**

Plymouth Sound is a broad natural break in the South West
Peninsula Coast Path, not as wide as the River Exe but still tinged
with that frontier spirit that saw the crossing of the water as 'going
to England'. In practical terms, the Duchy of Cornwall is left at
Cremyll where the ferry takes you over to Admiral's Hard and
the start of the South Devon Coast Path. But, whether continuing
or beginning the South West Way at this point, Plymouth is much
more than an urban interruption. Should you already be familiar
with it, then a No 7 city bus will take you beyond the built-up area
to an alternative Coast Path starting place. But if you do not know
Plymouth, then whether you arrive on foot, by bus, train, car, or
by air, make some time to explore this exciting English seaport.

Plymouth, now a city of nearly a quarter of a million
inhabitants, began as a small town called Sudstone on the east
bank of the River Tamar. Sudstone, later Sutton, grew into the
three towns of Plymouth, Stonehouse and Devonport. Prosperity
came in the fourteenth century with the growth of the English
wool trade with the Continent and, as commerce and religion
used then to go hand in hand, there were fine ecclesiastical as well
as domestic buildings. Religion was ever-present, and pilgrims
left in thousands for Jerusalem and the shrines of Europe. There
were constant departures and visitations – religious, commercial,
military and naval. Of the many raids by the French, one
recorded in 1388 described how: '. . . certain Pyrats sailed about
the hauens of Cornewall and Deuonshire, doing in all places
much harme to the fishermen, and such ships as they found
unmanned they fiered. At length they entred Plimmouth Hauen,
where they brent certain great shippes, and a great part of the
towne.'

It was from Plymouth that Sir Francis Drake set out, and to
which he returned in 1580 in *Golden Hind* from the first voyage
round the world; and it was from Plymouth that many other
Elizabethan mariners, explorers and adventurers, including
Frobisher, Ralegh, Hawkins, Gilbert, and Grenville, set sail. On
Plymouth Hoe Drake heard of the approach of the Spanish
Armada and set out to intercept it, later recording that '. . . with

all their great, terrible ostentation, they did not, in all their sailing about England, as much as sink or take one ship, bark, pinnace or cockboat of ours, or even burn so much as one sheepcote in this land.' The expedition under the Earl of Essex to sack Cadiz sailed from Plymouth in 1596; 101 Pilgrim Fathers in 1620 left Sutton Pool in *Mayflower*, and when they built their settlement in Massachusetts Bay they called it New Plymouth. The city has sent men to almost every part of the globe on missions both warlike and peaceful through the centuries. Captain Cook sailed in 1768 from Plymouth on his first voyage to the Antipodes, and to Plymouth Sir Francis Chichester returned after his solo circumnavigation of the world in 1967.

Walk up one of the narrow streets leading to the Hoe, and from the greensward at the top there is the spectacular sight of Plymouth Sound, Drake's Island, the River Plym or Cattewater to the east, and the River Tamar or Hamoaze to the west. Standing on the Hoe is Smeaton's lighthouse (1769), taken from the Eddystone Rock and re-erected here in 1882. There is a splendid view of Plymouth, both the old city and the new one which rose from the ruins left by heavy German bombing in the Second World War, from the top of the Civic Centre that houses a glass-walled restaurant and the Tourist Information Office (tel: 68000).

2 Plymouth to the River Yealm

Should you choose to walk through Plymouth from the Cremyll Ferry Landing, the most interesting route is by way of the docks and the Hoe to where the South Devon Coastal Path proper begins in the narrow streets of Turnchapel. From here it is a climb past Stamford Fort, one of the ten 'Palmerston Forts', built in the 1860s to protect the Royal Navy's base at Plymouth. From whom? From the French, of course! It is now a Holiday Centre and is perhaps in need of protection itself. Pass the Coast Guard lookout which stands on the clifftop to the right, and you come to Jennycliff Bay where the number 7 bus comes by way of Jennycliff Lane from Plymouth. In the summer there is also the open-top service 53 from Plymouth, which carries on further to Bovisand.

The Path continues along the road to Staddon Heights, where it leaves it to follow the coastline along the cliff. Inland is another gigantic fort, Staddon Fort, and between it and a golf-course there stands a wall built in 1883, 80 ft at the highest point, as the safety stop of a rifle-range. The next of the Palmerston Forts is Bovisand, partnered by Picklecombe Fort over on the Cornish side of the Sound. Both Forts lie just inside the line of the mile-long Plymouth Breakwater (1812–44) and the Breakwater Fort, and they guarded the approaches to the Naval base and the city, which are further protected deeper into the Sound by Drake's or St Nicholas's Island.

Bovisand is now the Fort Bovisand Underwater Centre, Plymouth Ocean Projects Ltd, and it houses, among other organizations, the British Sub-Aqua Club National Centre, the Devon Marine Centre, the Joint Services Sub-Aqua Diving Centre, the North-East London Polytechnic Field Centre, and the Plymouth Polytechnic Underwater Unit. One of those organizations may even be waymarking a submarine Coast Path!

Between Heybrook Bay and Wembury Point the Path runs directly below the green-plastic-covered wire fences of the shore battery commissioned in 1956 as HMS *Cambridge*. When the guns are practise-firing the Coast Path is closed, but there is a diversion through the Royal Navy establishment which makes it necessary to go around the inland limits of the naval base. Beyond the enclosed area the cliff opens out into a field and there are vegetable patches further inland. When the tide is out there is a large expanse of flat rocks and greyish sand, and there are also warning signs about the erosion of the Coast Path. Some of those flat rocks are fine to bathe from, but there are other rocks, both flat and pointed, under the surface so take care when diving. It is also sometimes difficult to get a firm hold of the smooth rock when coming out of the water. I once swam there on a September evening when the sea was like watered silk, shot with green and blue, and on the path eastwards was a refreshing crop of blackberries – sloes, too, if you have a masochistic taste for shrivelling of the taste buds.

Half a mile offshore lies the Great Mew Stone, an inhospitable-looking pyramidal rock that has in fact been

Going down to Wembury

inhabited at various times. In 1744 a man was sentenced to be
transported there for seven years, and he lived there with his
family without once coming to the mainland. When he did return
his daughter stayed on there, married, and had three children
before her husband was drowned – so the useful *Wembury
Footpath and General Guide* tells us – after falling off the rock into
the sea. In the early years of the nineteenth century a man called
Samuel Wakeham made his home on the Mew Stone and catered
for pioneer walkers of the Coast Path. He advertised in the *South
Devon Monthly Museum:* 'If any genteelman what likes a wark, he
can wark to the shoar at Wembury, and if they holds up there
white pockethanchecuffs for a signal, an ile cum off in me bote
and fetch them to the island for two pence . . .' But Sam dabbled
in smuggling too, and got his rowing orders back to the mainland.

Between Wembury Beach (to which a number 64 bus runs
from Plymouth) and Wembury village there stands on the cliff a
famous landmark for sailors which lines up with the Great Mew
Stone – Wembury parish church, dedicated to St Werburgh,

originally Wereburge, a Saxon saint. It was offshore here that the men of Devon fought and defeated the Danes in AD 851.

Some of the church's fifteenth-century architecture managed to survive nineteenth-century restoration, and over the south porch there remains a fragment of a Norman pier. Of two large and imposing monuments inside the church, one is to Sir John Hele who died in 1608. Serjeant-at-Law to Elizabeth I and James I, he took part in the trial of Sir Walter Ralegh and is depicted here in his legal robes, lying down propped on one elbow, his recumbent wife beside him, their daughter seated in a chair and their eight sons kneeling below. The other monument is to Lady Narborough who died in 1678. She was wife to an admiral and is shown kneeling on top of a great bulbous tomb supported by four white marble lions and surrounded by iron railings. The poor girl was only twenty, had been married less than a year, and is recorded as having died, while pregnant, 'of a mighty cough'.

This churchyard, sloping southwards towards the sea like a vineyard, has many tombstones with interesting inscriptions. Down from the church are the remains of a mill, in operation until the end of the last century, said to be on a site dating back to Saxon times. From here the Blackstone Rocks run out into the sea for $\frac{1}{4}$ mile, and are exposed at low tide.

The Coast Path goes up and behind Wembury church into National Trust land. There are a number of signposted footpaths, and an excellent guide to them, with a map, is published by Wembury Parish Council and may be bought from the Clerk to the Council, Channel View, Down Thomas, Plymouth (tel: Plymouth 862491). The Coast Path signs have the official yellow arrow on them and the Path crosses a lane and stays with the public footpath to Brownhill Lane. New, Scandinavian-looking houses in gleaming white lie on the left, just before a kissing-gate into a pasture leading to a lane with a high hedge on the right and houses behind fences to the left. This in turn leads into a narrow lane where I found the signs somewhat confusing, because one yellow arrow points up the lane and the other points in the opposite direction and there is no indication as to which way to go. I was misled initially by a delightfully

Newton Ferrers, at the mouth of the Yealm

garrulous old self-appointed guide, but the official Path goes along the top of the cliff, a fine walk looking across to the heavily wooded and rocky banks on the other side of the estuary of the River Yealm – the 'Yam'. This is Warren Point.

The Path runs down the slope of the river-bank, past an old Life-Saving Apparatus House (the method was the firing of rockets carrying lines) and past two cottages, to the steps where the ferry crosses to Newton Ferrers or direct to the Coast Path at Noss Mayo (May–September, 0900–1700, all week). When you get there, shout across the water or wave – even better, telephone before arrival to the ferrymen (Len Carter and Son, Plymouth (0752) 872210). The alternative, in other seasons or from choice, is to walk up-river and round by Yealmpton at the top of the estuary. A thatched cottage in 'Yampton' is said to have inspired Sarah Martin of the squire's family to write and publish, in 1805, the story of Mother Hubbard, supposedly based on the housekeeper at that time at Kitley, the house of the Martin family. The walk round by Yealmpton is about 10 miles – pleasant, but a long detour. It is only a small detour to explore the delightful twin villages of Newton and Noss, divided by Newton Creek filled with sailing craft, and whose fishermen's cottages are set against the thick ilex woods that crowd down from the sides of the creek to the harbour.

3 The Yealm to the Erme

Turn right from the Noss ferry-landing, along a footpath that leads into a broad lane along the edge of Ferry Wood, rising to the left in hawthorn, sycamore, and rhododendron. To the right is a hedge, beyond which the ground falls sharply down to the inlet on the other side of which the walker has travelled on the way from Wembury to Warren Point and Newton Ferrers. There are outcrops of red Devonian rock in the reddish soil, and beech trees seem to grow directly out of them.

This wide Path climbs past the old Coast Guard cottages and comes out into the open with gorse on both sides and some pasture and cultivated fields inland. Down on the shore, dark jagged rocks lie diagonally to the waves, and from Mouthstone Point to Gara Point there is fine clifftop walking with magnificent views – back, to the Great Mew Stone and beyond Plymouth Sound to the Cornish coast; eastward and ahead, across Bigbury Bay to Bolt Head and Prawle Point: a satisfying vista of where you have been and where you are going.

From Gara Point the Path turns from south-south-west to east-south-east to cross The Warren. There is a tiny detour around Warren Cottage, one of the most pleasantly isolated houses on the south coast of England, set snugly with its back into the hillside and presenting in the best possible way to sun and sea the garden bright with flowers – I noticed in particular the fuschia and montbretia in strong profusion. Just beyond Warren Cottage the Path is guarded to seaward by a drystone wall, at the end of which the Path takes a right-hand fork. There is a sign, but

Yealm Mouth, from the Noss Mayo side

Yealm Mouth, from the Newton Ferrers side

it could easily be missed should one be unwise or unfortunate enough to travel there in mist or at night. The first human habitation after Warren Cottage is the Coast Guard building; from a distance it looks as if there is a polluting cascade of rubbish, mostly white paper, broken glass and bright tin cans, but when one gets there it turns out to be chips of rock frothing down from the somewhat battered wall to seaward of the track. The Path climbs first over Snellings Down and then over Netton Down. Both downs are boulder-strewn, and the cliffs here are scree-streaked and sloping, pink with foxglove, while in the chinks of the rocks to the left of the path grow mauve thrift and tiny white sedum.

After rounding Stoke Point, the Path opens out into a green road, originally a 'pleasure' carriage drive built by Barings the bankers, wooded on either side with horse-chestnut, elder, oak, rhododendron and hawthorn, with bramble and black bryony, and, in one place, a mass of gorse in an overgrown quarry. To the right, and lying well below, is a caravan park which is just about as close to the rocks and sea as any caravan park on this walk. The Path comes out at a road junction where, at the end of a short garden-path to the left, is the PSDC Ltd Shop and Café, presumably the Co-Op shop for the Co-Op caravan site below. I was amused by the ancient, dark-red privy-type, tongue-and-groove wooden telephone kiosk beside the shop.

It is worth making a short detour down a tree-lined road, probably an estate avenue of nearby Stoke House, to the partially ruined and disused church of St Peter the Poor Fisherman, Revelstoke. A notice explains that 'this ancient church is maintained by the Redundant Churches Fund, St Andrew by the Wardrobe, Queen Victoria Street, London EC4 with monies provided by Parliament, by the Church of England, by the gifts of the public . . . no longer required for regular worship, remains consecrated to the service of God. Please respect it accordingly.' On passing through the doorway into the church I found that it was roofless and that the aisle was being renovated. In fact, the whole church was being restored, and although the churchyard was full of weeds, autumn crocuses flowered reassuringly on some of the graves.

Looking east along the Coast Path on the clifftop, from Revelstoke churchyard

In the nave, then open to the sky for the most part, is a
tombstone in the extreme south-east corner said to be that of a
pirate. The inscription is nearly impossible to read, having been
tramped over for several generations, and all I could make out
was the word 'anno' and a 'D' cut the wrong way round. Easier to
read is a tablet on the wall 'sacred to the memory of Miriam, the
beloved wife of Captain William Kingcome, who departed this life
after a short illness on board the ship Scrabjee Jamsetjee
Jeejeebhoy at the entrance to the River Hooghly, January 1st
1867, aged 27 years'. Of what disease did Miriam die? Would she
have survived had that exotically named ship put her ashore?
There is somewhere there a story from the days of Imperial India
that would surely have intrigued my late friend Paul Scott, author
of *The Raj Quartet* and *Staying On*.

Looking east from the road up from the church, the Coast Path
can be seen climbing, wide and green, along the clifftop on the far
side of this indentation of the coast. It is reached at that same
road junction where the detour to the church begins. From there
it runs as a wide track to Beacon Hill, on which stands the ruins of
Lady Baring's carriage-drive 'Tea House'. Beyond Beacon Hill
the Path leaves the green road, which turns sharply inland, and
runs along the clifftop in an easy up-and-down way towards St
Anchorite's Rock, a great boulder that stands out from its
downland surroundings, an unexpected, abrupt, 30-ft rock rising
from the ground. Was the holy anchorite really a Stylite who lived
atop his rock in lieu of a pillar?

I encountered some difficulty around here, because I was
about to follow a path running inland and then was tempted to
follow another marked 'Private' which seemed to go in the right
direction; but in fact the Coast Path turns very sharply to the
right, almost loses itself in a coppice, and then emerges into a low
pasture where some balks of timber span a narrow stream. In the
middle of this field there is a Coast Path sign – you have to watch
out for it – followed by a climb up a steep slope to a stile where
there is a mark that sends you almost to the foot of St Anchorite's
Rock.

The South West Way: a Complete Guide to the Coastal Path, 1981
edition, states that: 'There is no coastal path from seaward of
Battisborough House to Erme Mouth as yet. Devon County
Council were hopeful that the old coastal path would be
re-opened for Spring 1978 but at the time of writing it has still not
come to pass. . . . All we can say is that it will be an enormous
improvement over the present unpleasant and at times
dangerous walk on the road.' Hugh Westacott commented in the
second edition of his *Devon South Coast Path* (1977): 'Between
Battisborough Island and Mothecombe the official path makes an
irritating detour inland which includes more than a mile of road.
There is a perfectly practicable coastal path to Erme Mouth, but
although well used it appears not to be a right of way.'

I had intended to make the official trek around by the road, but
when I opened a gate for a tractor hauling bales of hay the farmer

driving it stopped, thanked me, and asked if I was heading for
Erme Mouth. When I said I was, he replied: 'You don't need to
take the road. Just follow the seaward side of that fence around
the copse, and when you get to the tall pine nearest to the clifftop
get through the fence and you'll find a path going down through
the trees that will bring you out near a boathouse. There is a gate
there to a path through some more trees and on to the road,
where you turn right down to the river – and you'd better hurry,'
looking at his watch, 'or the tide will have come in too far for you
to wade across.'

I followed his instructions to the letter, jogging the last few
hundred yards after I saw the incoming waves corrugating the
estuary and eating up swiftly the broad expanse of sand between
the rocks and cliffs. With trousers, boots and socks tied around
my neck I waded across – thigh-deep in the middle – with the
firm sand underfoot and the gentle yet insistent waves,
green-crowned with bladderwort, trying to push me up-river.
There was no sound but the swishing of the water, the cry of
gulls, and the murmur of a tractor ploughing across the red
hillside field on the far side of the estuary.

Once across, I had a swim and then climbed on to some rocks
where I could both watch the incoming afternoon tide and have
something to eat and drink. The tide moves very quickly and I
could see that it would be dangerous to try to cross when the
water is deeper and rougher than it was on that day. It is essential
to work out the times of the tides and to follow the notes given in
the *South West Way: a Complete Guide*. There is no ferry here at any
time, and for those who arrive when it is impossible to cross at the
point where the old ford used to be (no longer shown on OS maps
but formerly running from OS map ref. 614476 to map ref.
620478, i.e., from beside the Coast Guard cottages), there is a
detour nearly three miles up-river to Sequers Bridge, on the
A379 above Holbeton. This can be irritating, and involves some
eight miles of road-walking; but I have been to Holbeton on
another occasion and found it a pleasant village of narrow streets
of stone-and-thatch cottages, a former workhouse turned into a
pub called The Dartmoor Union, and a church set high above the

Looking east from the top of Beacon Hill, towards St Anchorite's Rock

houses, with a tower and spire over 100 ft high, dating from the
late thirteenth to the early fourteenth century. The interior has
sixteenth-century screens, impeccably restored in Victorian times
by an artist craftsman who faithfully copied the originals, and an
early seventeenth-century monument, identified by Pevsner as
belonging to the Hele family and incorporating the central figure
of a knight, and four tiers of kneeling figures.

4 The Erme to the Avon

Assuming that you have beaten the tide, the Coast Path continues
on the east bank of the Erme estuary at Wonwell – 'Wonnel' –
Beach, by going up to the right of the ruined cottage, between
hedges, to come out on open cliffs where there are some
vertiginous drops to the sea on the right of the Path, that often
seems to be perilously near to the cliff edge. It is so close in places
that care must be taken not to snag landward-side sleeves and
rucksacks on the barbed wire that hems the walker in tightly for
about two miles. Behind that sturdy fence is cultivated land, with
here and there a pasture where cows graze; but in general the

effect is of a windy, treeless, and even gorseless, tract. It is also one of steep gradients down to, and up from, little streams at Freshwater and Westcombe Beach. The path here can be treacherously slippery during and after rain or frost – difficult in a high wind, too, I imagine.

Bigbury-on-Sea comes into view along here or, rather, Burgh Island, pyramidal and connected to the mainland by Sandy Causeway which can be crossed at low tide, St Michael's Mount fashion. By the time I had walked the next half-mile and made the steep descent to Ayrmer Cove, the light was beginning to fail and a cool breeze was springing up, cool enough to dissuade me from sleeping on the beach or in the lee of a ruined building, where I had a short rest and brewed up. Then I walked inland for a mile, and found a bed in the village of Ringmore at the Journey's End Inn, an ancient and pleasant pub which takes its name from the title of the play which R.C. Sherriff wrote while he was staying there. Seekers after the true ale of England will find a fine selection there, some from the wood.

Before setting off on the Path next morning, I looked round Ringmore which is far enough from both the main road and the sea to have remained relatively untouched. Many of the cottages are thatched and the rich growth of flowers and vegetables in the gardens bears witness to the sheltered position Ringmore enjoys. All Hallows Church is mostly of the thirteenth century, and has a fourteenth-century chapel. During the Civil War the Royalist rector, William Lane, trained his parishioners to fight, placed guns in the fields overlooking the bridge that carries the main road over the River Avon, and set out to hold the village for the King. Parliamentary soldiers were sent by boat from Plymouth to Ayrmer Cove to storm the village and hang the rector, but when they got there William Lane was nowhere to be found. He was there all right – hidden in a tiny room in the tower of his church, where he remained for three months, subsisting on food and drink smuggled to him by his parishioners who were as loyal to their rector as they were to their King.

Ringmore is one of the prettiest villages in the district of the South Hams, an area that has been described as covering a wildly varying territory. It can be fairly defined as the country between the Plym in the west and the Dart in the east, bounded roughly on the northern edge by the Totnes-Avonwick road and from Avonwick to the Plym, and in the south, of course, by the sea. It is sheltered in the north by Dartmoor which gives it a mild climate, lush pastures and the South Devon breed of cattle that originated here. The South Hams are deeply indented by the estuaries of the rivers Yealm, Erme and Avon, and the salt water of Salcombe Harbour lies on the eastern edge. This is a self-contained and most attractive district, along whose southern border the Coast Path runs.

Less than a mile of easy walking brings you to Challaborough where there are shops, pubs, cafés, and a sandy beach. About half a mile further on is Bigbury-on-Sea, a modern bungaloid holiday development $1\frac{1}{2}$ miles from Bigbury village proper, which is inland. Bigbury-on-Sea has accommodation, food shops, a pub and a youth hostel, and buses in the summer season, the 99 to Plymouth and the 610 local bus to Modbury. When I was there it was crowded with holiday-makers, and I decided not to visit Burgh Island where there is the Pilchard pub, which dates from the fourteenth century, and a large hotel, formerly the home of a millionaire but now let out in holiday flats. The extraordinary machine that looks like something out of an early space film, is a tractor elevated on stilts which can cross to the island on the causeway through as much as nine feet of water. I was told that it was invented by a visitor, and had it not been going the other way when I spotted it, I could not have resisted a closer look at it. Because I was there at high tide, I could not take the route along the sands of the estuary to the point where the ferry crosses to Bantham, but had to climb up the busy road where the only way to avoid being squashed when two large lorries meet is to squeeze into the bank. At the top of the hill a path beside Mount Folly Farmhouse leads down the steep bank to the river at Cockleridge Strand.

5 **The Avon to Salcombe**

It is possible to wade across the Avon, but the conditions must be right and great care is needed. Above all, do not try to cross at what looks like the most likely spot at the mouth of the Avon, for there is a great rush of tide, both up and down. Take off from the end of a hedge that has some pine trees in it, and head for the flagpole in the middle of a castellated building on the opposite shore. The most up-to-date information about this and other ferries is in the *South West Way: a Complete Guide*, which is revised annually. Broadly speaking, the ferry operates for an hour in the morning and an hour in the afternoon, 1000–1100 and 1500–1600, Monday to Saturday, for two weeks at Easter and from 21 May to 29 September, and also on Sundays in July and August only. When the ferry is running, stand at the ferry point, shout 'Ferry!' and hope for the best.

I arrived at a time when I had an afternoon wait of more than two hours for the ferry, and rather longer for the tide to be low enough for wading. There was not enough depth of water to have a swim to help pass the time, so I walked up and down the shore in the sunshine and met Dr Mary Dixon who lives at Bantham on the other side and was about to cross in her boat with a friend. She told me that she would take me over if I would pay her tenpence to give to the ferryman, as she did not wish to seem a competitor. She also told me that the old building at the mouth of the Avon is not a water-mill, which I had thought it might be, but a building put up in Victorian times for use by salmon fishermen. It is always being photographed, frequently appears on calendars, and is described as an ancient monument. From beside it, a glance down at the Avon shows how dangerous it would be to try wading at this point.

On that afternoon Bantham was nearly asleep, except for the hollow hammering of some boat-repairing and the starting-up of cars outside the Sloop at closing time. There is accommodation at the Sloop Inn, a good place to stay on this quiet Avon estuary outside the holiday season.

The Coast Path runs parallel to the estuary around a little north-facing peninsula, following the line of the cliffs that look

The salmon fishermen's hut at Bantham

down on Bantham Sands, where the Path turns southwards. This
is easy walking, and for more than a mile the Path is just to
seaward of Thurlestone Golf Course. Thurlestone takes its name
from the 'pierced stone' that stands on the shore. Here again
there is excellent bathing from good sands, and everything that
goes with a popular summer resort. The modern buildings to
landward of the golf-course are not the village of Thurlestone,
which is half a mile inland and is one of those places that give
South Devon its reputation as the Riviera of England. There are
palm trees, and in summer the gardens of the thatched houses
are bursting with brightness. The noble red sandstone church
dates from the thirteenth century and has a Norman font in red
sandstone; it also has a fine 1658 Stephens memorial in which the
family is shown kneeling, in the Elizabethan tradition.

  At the end of the golf-course the Path is signposted as going

The 'pierced stone' at Thurlestone

around the back of a block of flats called Links Court, because of a cliff-fall which took most of the road. But it still left enough room for a footpath. Perhaps this is dangerous, and further falls may occur, but the 1981 *South West Way: a Complete Guide* suggests it is safe to take the old Path and that the diversion around Links Court is illegal anyway. Assuming that one does take the diversion, it emerges on to a macadam road, and a line of houses is passed, after which there is a sign to the Coast Path by way of a bridge over a reedy little swamp called South Milton Ley, a refuge for rare marsh- and sea-birds when breeding. The bridge has railings and is taken across the Ley on stout round pillars that make it look like a main-line railway-bridge in miniature. The Path carries on upwards, easy to follow, between gorse on the seaward side and pastures beyond a barbed-wire fence to the left.

Hope Cove

It is a wide path and the walker is not cramped between wire and clifftop.

From this path Bolt Tail is nearly always in sight, and is soon followed by a view down to the twin villages of Outer and Inner Hope. The Outer is a modern growth, much of it set up to cater for summer visitors to Hope Cove; the Inner is the old village. Perhaps they represent Hope Present and Hope Past. Inner Hope has remained more or less inviolate, with fishermen's cottages around two squares, and a sense that the same kind of life goes on there in winter as it has always done – perhaps as it did when the Armada vessel *St Peter the Great* was wrecked below Bolt Tail; or when, two centuries later, the frigate HMS *Ramillies* was lost in 1760 with all but 26 of her crew of 734.

There is a steady climb up the bracken-bordered Path to the

top of Bolt Tail and the Coast Guard Station with its tall wireless mast inside the earthworks of a prehistoric promontory fort.

Near the mast is a monolith of sturdy stone put up by the Devon Fund to make an appeal for the National Trust, 'which needs money for its work protecting the beautiful countryside of Devon' – when I was there, the top of the hill was golden with gorse. The Coast Path runs, for the next five miles, to Bolt Head through National Trust land high along the clifftops, giving some of the most satisfying walking on the South Devon Coast Path.

Wireless masts rise from the top of Bolberry Down, and a road that was built during World War II leads to the Port Light, a small, square, flat-roofed hotel and restaurant. There it is, seemingly in the middle of nowhere – a welcoming place, whether for coffee, a drink, a meal, or a room for the night. Rooms do get booked up in advance, but as it is an ideal place to stay on this coast try your luck (Michael and Mary Piggott, The Port Light, Kingsbridge 561384). The traveller is always welcome – I sat with Michael in the kitchen while the plaster was flying in the new extension. There are many stories of West Way walkers who have called here, some with children on their backs and some with retirement-pension books in their pockets.

Inland from the Coast Path east of Bolberry Down there is almost a moorland landscape, with outcrops of rock close to the broad path that runs between bracken and gorse. From the highest point one looks down the steep descent to Soar Mill Cove and inland to Hazel Tor, a large block of rock sitting stolidly in this landscape of deep valleys segmented into smaller valleys. Just beyond Lantern Rock, a Coast Path sign points to Bolberry Down in the west and to Bolt Head in the east. These cliffs rise to 400 ft.

There is a steep descent to the small and sheltered Soar Mill Cove, and it can be slippery. The rocks offshore are the Priest and the Clerk; further out to sea is the Ham Stone where in 1936 the four-masted *Herzogin Cecilie* ran ashore under full sail, with a cargo of wheat from Australia. The crew and some of the cargo were saved, and some weeks later she was towed round to Starehole Cove on the western shore of the Salcombe Estuary, where she broke up in 1939. This was a sea story that caught the

Kingsbridge Estuary, looking inland

imagination of the British press and public, as did that of Captain
Carlsen and *Flying Enterprise* a decade later. On these same rocks
in the 1880s a tea-clipper, *Hallowe'en*, went ashore and broke up
in a gale, casting great banks of tea-leaves on the Devon shore.

Less than a mile inland from Soar Mill Cove, where I found
safe and calm swimming early one morning, there is the Soar Mill
Cove Hotel with a restaurant and a tea and ice-cream kiosk at the
head of the combe leading to the cove. A young man called Mike
told me that he was blocked in during the heavy snows of early
1978, and that when the thaw came a river of water broke
through the glacier-like ice which had been a gigantic drift in
front of the hotel. The hotel itself was spared because of the lie of
the land.

From Soar Mill Cove to Bolt Head the Path is easy going along
the clifftop, and one is constantly surprised and one's imagination
stirred along the way by the fantastic shapes of the jagged rocks.
All this is fortunately in the safe-keeping of the National Trust,

and one wonders what horrendous development might have taken place had it not been. The Path is straightforward and simple to follow, but at Bolt Head there is a choice of routes into Salcombe: one is an inland short cut by way of East Soar Farm, but do not take it, pleasant though it is, because the clifftop walk is so worthwhile. To take the top path follow the sign 'South Sands via Bolt Head' which brings you down to Starehole Bay and then up again and around Sharp Tor. The rocks along Bolt Head – particularly early in the morning or at sunset – are hatchet-faced totems, shadows cast by witches, goblins, dragons according to tricks of light and state of mind. Beyond Starehole Bay the Path enters some woods, leads to a gate, and goes up some steps into Courtenay Walk and the approaches of Salcombe.

6 Salcombe

In the mid-nineteenth century, the Earl of Devon, whose family had owned the land hereabouts for centuries, lived chiefly at Powderham Castle, the family seat near Exeter. He had built for himself a 'marine residence' called The Moult above Salcombe, between North Sands and South Sands. It was when the Earl's eldest son, Viscount Courtenay, lived here that the path was cut to Bolt Head and named the Courtenay Walk. J.A. Froude, the historian, lived later at The Moult, and while staying there Tennyson is said to have conceived the idea of his poem 'Crossing the Bar', as he often went sailing out of Salcombe Harbour 'across the bar'.

When the Great Western branch-line from South Brent to Kingsbridge was opened in 1893, Lord Devon sold much of his land above Salcombe for development and for the houses that would be required when Salcombe, under the blessing of steam, became a big town. Some houses were built but the branch-line never arrived. On one of the plots a villa was constructed by a local builder who called it Sharpitor, after one of the craggy rocks or sharp tors to the west. Edric Hopkins lived there as tenant until 1901, when he bought the freehold and added an extra couple of acres to the land on which he laid out a garden and planted a variety of exotic trees and shrubs. In 1913 he sold both house and land to G.M. Vereker who demolished the house and built the much larger one that stands there today. Vereker bought more land, and he and his wife continued planting gardens on the same lines as the previous owners. After his death in 1928, the property was bought by Otto Christop Jos Gerard Ludwig Overbeck, a research chemist descended from a Dutch family who had many interests and was an omnivorous collector. When Overbeck died in 1937 he left his house, grounds, and collection to the National Trust for use as a youth hostel, park, and museum which it has been ever since – apart from a brief period during the war when it was used for billeting troops. The youth hostel can take 72 guests at a time, and the museum includes a typical South Hams cottage parlour of the last century, agricultural implements, many shipbuilding mementoes, and a natural history collection. The garden looks over the sea and Salcombe Estuary, and, as frost is almost unknown here, among the rarer sub-tropical specimens at Sharpitor are a Japanese banana tree, palms from China planted by Overbeck, the maidenhair tree also from China, and the *Gingko biloba*, a survivor from the coal age and the oldest species of tree in existence.

The Courtenay Walk, leading to Sharpitor, is paved and tree-bordered, with oak predominating, and chestnut and plane covering the ground that drops sharply to the sea on one side, and rises equally sharply on the other with thick undergrowth and a carpet of ivy, dog's mercury and brambles. At the end of Courtenay Walk there is an abrupt turn to the left marked with a yellow arrow and above it the sign, 'YHA and to Sharpitor Upper Cliff Path, National Trust', and below it, 'The National Trust, Sharpitor Gardens'.

I saw a YHA sign, 'Beds available – Boys, 20. Girls, 20', but perhaps that means the number available on that day as the official guide gives the number of beds as 72. I was not there at a time when the Hostel was open – a note on the door stated, 'Hostel opens at 5 p.m. Members arriving early may leave their kit in the cycle shed opposite the main gate'. The view from the terrace over conifers and beeches to the sea gives an impression of the Mediterranean – the luxuriant growth, the blue of the sea,

Sharpitor House and gardens, with sub-tropical plants, at Salcombe

the sense of fertility in the soil and the mildness in the air.
Margaret Willy in her book *The South Hams* (Hale, 1955) writes of
a nineteenth-century clergyman living on the Portlemouth side of
the estuary who said that Salcombe from across the water always
reminded him of Algiers.

Leaving aside heady comparisons, Salcombe is not particularly
interesting architecturally – not even a mosque in mirage. There
is a large church (1843), many Victorian houses, and the majority
of the shops, and the town centre itself, are crammed along Fore
Street and the edge of the harbour. In summer Salcombe is
packed with visitors and at pretty well all seasons it is well stocked
with sailing enthusiasts. There are good pubs – The King's Head
in Fore Street is one of them – and many restaurants. Historically,
Salcombe used to build boats and its harbour flourished due to

foreign trade and fishing. At the eastern end of North Sands Bay
stands Fort Charles or Salcombe Castle, one of those many South
Coast forts built by Henry VIII against the French and Spanish
threat. It was patched up, and held out in the spring of 1646
against Parliamentary forces. Commanded by Sir Edmund
Fortescue, High Sheriff of Devon, and named Fort Charles in
Royalist defiance, it was reduced by Parliamentary shelling from
East Portlemouth after a siege of four months. Fortescue
surrendered on more or less his own terms, which included
freedom of religious belief for the defenders and Fortescue's
retention of the key to the fort. They marched out, 66 men and
two laundresses, and took the 10-mile-long road to Fallapit,
where they fired three volleys before laying down their arms –
colours still flying, royal coat of arms displayed – and were then
disbanded.

7 Salcombe to Prawle Point

The vagaries of ferries are one of the time-wasting hazards of the
South Devon Coast Path, but Salcombe, one of the most southerly
resorts and the largest yachting centre in England, is a blissful
exception. The ferry is run by Limhart Ltd of Bradford in
Yorkshire – I do not know what significance there is in that – and
runs throughout the year, seven days a week and at half-hourly
intervals. Do not get there before 0700 or after 1950 in winter, or
after 2030 in summer; on Sundays it is an hour later starting, and
an hour earlier finishing in the evening.

   The ferry crosses to East Portlemouth, a rival to Salcombe in
the Middle Ages. Now it is a village with no pretension to being
anything more than a charming place, with a church tower that
dominates the surrounding landscape. The church is dedicated to
St Winwaloe (or St Onolaus), a sixth-century Breton missionary
who crossed to Cornwall and Devon; this is the only dedication to
this saint in England. The church is fifteenth-century, but was
drastically restored in 1881. There is a fine sixteenth-century
screen on which are painted, in scarlet and gold, very small
figures, which include St Winwaloe in a white gown and red cloak
and holding a church.

Look for this chilling epitaph in the churchyard:

Here lieth the body of Richard Jarvis of Rickham in this
Parish, who departed this life the 25th day of May, 1782, aged
77.
> Through poisons strong he was cut off
> And brought to death at last.
> It was by his apprentice girl
> On whom there's sentence past.
> Oh may all people warning take,
> For she was burned at the stake.

What story lies behind that? If she was burned and not hanged
for the murder of her master, it was because she was deemed to
be a witch. And why did she kill him? If she did.

In the church there is a montage headed, 'St Guenolé of
Brittany' – the same St Winwaloe of Portlemouth – and a sketch
map of Brittany showing Landevennec where St Guenolé had
founded a monastery in AD 485. In AD 914 the abbey was sacked
and burned by the Normans, but by 1268 it had been rebuilt, and
the first rector of East Portlemouth seems to have been appointed
in AD 1300–1400. In 1646 the screen of the church was damaged
by Roundheads who tried to set fire to it.

The monks of Landevennec left there at the time of the
French Revolution and lived in exile in Wales, returning home
only in 1903. In 1965 the new abbey church of Landevennec was
consecrated: there is a photograph of it in East Portlemouth
Church, and the Breton Valley of the Aulne in which it lies looks
very much like the valley of the Erme in Devon.

After climbing the steps from the ferry, follow the road east
through woods by way of Small's Cove and Mill Bay where there
are sandy beaches. From Mill Bay take the footpath nearest to the
estuary shore, which brings you to Rickham Common, a
variegated landscape of cultivated fields, gorse patches, and
blackthorn thickets, with bracken and ragwort reaching an
amazing height.

The Path undulates between outcrops of rock clasped by

A lookout tower on the way to the Gara Rock Hotel

brambles, and just before reaching Gara Rock it is joined by the other path from Mill Bay. Down on the shore is Rudder Cove and Abraham's Hole – two names which provoke speculation as to their origin, one so nautical and the other so Biblical.

Making a small detour to look at the Gara Rock Hotel is worthwhile. It was originally a Coast Guard station and became an hotel in 1907. Now there are 44 bedrooms and some private suites or flats for family occupation (tel: Salcombe 2342). This is the last place for refreshments before reaching Hallsands, nearly 10 miles on.

The Coast Path passes through thick bracken growing right to the edge of the low brown and orange cliffs that drop to the greenish-grey rock lying below in great flat slabs. When the tide is out there is an expanse of fine sand called Seacombe Sand, and there is access to it by following the path downwards alongside a small stream. The Path continues through this National Trust land along the top of Deckler's Cliff, and curving inland along the headland of Pig's Nose. It becomes very porcine along here, because just beyond Pig's Nose is Ham Stone and Ham Stone Cove, and the next headland is called Gammon Head. Immediately to the east of Gammon Head is Maceley Cove, reached by a very steep path if you feel like a swim in calm water sheltered from the west wind. Just beyond the stream that falls to the sea at Maceley Cove, is a path to the left leading to the village of East Prawle, a little over a mile away at the end of a steady climb. The Path to Prawle Point follows the clifftop.

Prawle Point is the most southerly point of Devon and its name is Old English for 'Look Out Hill': it was a Lloyd's signal station before becoming a Coast Guard station which is still in operation. Off Prawle Point is an island with the simple and aristocratic name 'The Island'. I believe that it has no other name, but it is known very well to migrating birds and those who observe them. The South West Way Notes on the Salcombe to Torcross section of the Coast Path state that this was one of the traditional habitats of the peregrine falcon, 'and with the bird making a come-back to the South-West, one can but hope that one day it will return'.

8 Prawle Point to Start Point

Rounding Prawle Point a very different coastline and landscape come into sight. In place of the stark rocky cliffs of the coast between Salcombe Estuary and Prawle Point, there are shelves or raised beaches formed at a time when the sea level was higher than it is today, and the original cliffs are now about half a mile inland. The Coast Path tacks sharply down to the fields along these raised beaches, passing in front of the row of Coast Guard cottages and on to the edge of the cliff again, passing over stone stiles, and through gates, to Langerstone Point. Here there is a good view of where you have come from, including a clear sight of the hole that the sea has worn through the rock under Prawle Point. The trail then goes slightly inland and there is a path down to Horsley Cove, a steep up-and-down detour on the kind of hot day when one feels most inclined to take it.

Continuing along the Coast Path, with or without having taken time off for a bathe, one passes through more gates, in front of a large house, and through an area whose market-garden history is proclaimed by the skeleton of a large greenhouse. Philip Carter, South West Way secretary, told me that two brothers used to run it very efficiently but when one died and the other grew old there was nobody to carry on. It is sad to see this garden, south-facing and in such a protected spot, now abandoned.

From here on the Path becomes more enclosed, with much gorse and bramble on both sides, as it gets closer again to the sea. Offshore is Ballsaddle Rock which, when I passed along there, served as a high-rise tenement for gulls. A strange name; and I also wondered how Stinking Cove got its name. A beached whale or dolphin, a cargo of guano from a wrecked ship?

The Path descends to Lannacombe, and then climbs through pasture, with bracken and brambles on either side; after half a mile or so the rocks to the landward side rise sharply in crags overhanging the path – or so it seems. The Path along here is marked on the 25,000 map as 'The Narrows' and one of the crags is named the 'King's Head Rock' – although I looked, looked away and then looked again, without finding any outline that suggested to me a human cranium of any kind, let alone an uneasy one that wears a crown. Great Mattiscombe Sand is the grandiose name of the next beach, more often known to walkers and locals as just Mattiscombe or Matchcombe Beach. Just before the shore levels out into the sands, there is a collection of jagged rocks, called the Pinnacles, that rise from the sea like sculptures.

This part of the coast is not short of fanciful names. After Mattiscombe comes Peartree Cove, Frenchman's Rock (did he land on it, cling to it, or was he marooned on it?), Barler Rock, Peartree Point and, round the other side towards the Start, Raven's Cove, Gull Island, Bullock Cove, Foxhole Cove, and Crab and Crater. Walking around Peartree Point, one is again hemmed in by crags to landward and jagged cliffs falling to a churning race; and then, rounding the Point, the Start comes into view. The Path from here to Hallsands is waymarked with splashes of blue paint.

'Start' is derived from Anglo-Saxon *steort* or 'tail' and this tail of land projects in descending steps, and treacherously continues into the sea by the Black Stone, to run north-east from Start Bay as the Skerries Bank (the only Norse name in Devon, by the way, unless you count the island of Lundy). The Start, the Black Stone and the Skerries have seen countless shipwrecks, both before and since the lighthouse was built here in 1836. Now it has a fixed red-light warning of the Skerries Bank, and a revolving light giving three flashes every ten seconds, visible for 20 miles. There was a particularly terrible series of shipwrecks off the Start in March 1891 when blizzards swept the West Country. In the late afternoon of 9 March of that year, the steamer *Marana*, bound for Colombo, struck the Black Stone and lost all but three of her crew of 26 or 28; and later that same night the Valparaiso-bound iron sailing-ship *Dryad* went ashore just to the north-east of Start Point, with the loss of the entire crew of 22. Two schooners, *Lunesdale* and *Lizzie Ellen*, were also lost in Start Bay during this blizzard.

I have never seen Start Point in rough weather, but it is easy to imagine, looking down those quartz-veined rocks to the foam-topped breakers of Start Race, what menace and fury are aroused there by storms.

9 Start Point to Dartmouth

Just before reaching Start lighthouse there is a cave, and beyond it are three toadstool-shaped rocks. The Path becomes steeper and the bracken thins out where the rock is closer to the surface. On the way beyond the lighthouse there is a stout limestone wall on the top of the cliff, a wall roofed with concrete. On the other side of that wall, where the cliff drops quite sharply to the sea, sheep graze – sheep that are peach- or apricot-coloured from the red soil, whose colour has been diluted by rain on the wool.

On some maps, including the 25,000 South Devon Outdoor Leisure Map, and also in Hugh Westacott's *Devon South Coast Path*, the official Path is marked as turning off left before the lighthouse, to cross the spine of the ridge and come out on the road leading to the lighthouse. But, to avoid walking both down and back along this road, one can keep closer to the cliffs and come out just by the lighthouse and then take the macadam

lighthouse road for half a mile to the car-park at the top, on Start
Farm, from which there is a fine view north over Start Bay. The
car-park is to landward of a wire fence, and the Coast Path
continues along the cliffs outside the fence. I was confused by two
Coast Path signs at the car-park, but one was a mistake and the
South West Way Association took steps to have it removed. There
is a plaque here that states: 'Devon Trust for Nature
Conservation and Sir Ralph Newman Park Nature Reserve.
Please help to protect flowers and wildlife.'

The Path is waymarked in blue, and from it there is one of the
most extensive views ahead along the Coast Path, which goes
down gently from here to Hallsands, about which there is a
curious history. The village suffered from that great blizzard of
1891 which I mentioned earlier, and then, between 1897 and
1901, shingle was dredged from the area for the construction of
Keyham Docks at Devonport. It was believed that the tides would
replace the shingle that had been removed. But it was not
replaced. The beach, which was now lowered by some 15ft, had
previously acted as a natural barrier to the sea, protecting the two
rows of cottages that had inexplicably been built on the former
raised beach. In 1903 a storm took away the outer row of houses,
and Sidney Heath wrote in *The South Devon and Dorset Coast* (1910)
that Hallsands was then 'a village that came prominently into
public notice two or three years ago in consequence of the sudden
subsidence of several of the houses near the sea owing to the
removal of the shore shingle. The unfortunate inhabitants
petitioned the Government against any further removal, or it is
probable that the whole of the village would have slipped into the
sea.' Which it did, when the gale of January 1917 swept over the
sea wall that had been built, and undermined the remaining
houses so that they were abandoned. The new village was rebuilt
at a sensible distance inland. The little that remains of the old
village may be seen by making a detour down the track marked
'Ruined Village, Road Closed'.

The new cottages, in which the refugees from shingle-theft and
tide-invasion were rehoused, look across the valley and, so A.G.
Collings writes in the excellent Salcombe to Torcross Notes for

the South West Way, 'A willow grove along the stream provided the withies from which crab pots have been made for generations – the art still survives despite competition from synthetic pots'.

According to the state of the tides, there is a choice between walking from Hallsands along the beach for the next two miles to Torcross Point, or walking along the top of the cliffs over Tinsey Head. I met with an incoming tide so I took the top route – not out of piety and slavish devotion to the 'official' Path, but mostly because I find more than a mile of seashore walking rather boring anyway. The clifftop path is a pleasant pastoral walk, with hedges and blackberries and a pair of magpies who seemed to be putting on an exhibition game of tag just in front of me for a couple of hundred yards.

A mile beyond Hallsands is Beesands – a row of houses and the Cricket Inn. This used to be a fishing village, noted for its hauls of crab and lobster, but the fishermen who still live there now work mostly out of Dartmouth. The pilchards caught by Beesands fisherman used to be stored in cellars, now disused, which are passed by the Coast Path just before it climbs past a large caravan site, bright in summer with all the vivid plastic seaside holiday aids and glumly withdrawn in winter like a centre for unemployed garden gnomes hibernating in deflated beach mattresses. Inland is a triangular sheet of water called Widdicombe Ley, which the owner of the Torcross Hotel had dug and stocked with fish. German bombers unleashed an air raid on unsuspecting Beesands in 1943 and did considerable damage.

Tides again play a part in what the walker does next, for beyond Widdicombe Ley it is possible at low tide to walk along the shore, despite the notice to the effect that the foreshore is private beyond a house called Sunnydale. The Coast Path itself climbs to skirt around the top of a disused slate quarry and then drops to the village of Torcross. I have not taken the alternative route along the shore and I will again quote A.G. Collings's Notes, which point out something important: 'A glance at the map suggests there is another public footpath seaward of the quarry, but this is not so. It is in fact two separate paths – the cart track of the quarry long since eroded by the sea, and a path out from

Torcross at the top of the 100-ft cliffs, with no connection between the two. However, at low tide one can follow along the shore, passing the entrance to the quarry – abandoned to nature long ago, and when past the Cove Guest House go up the steps, inland of the two houses on the point, then bear right and down the steps to emerge on the sea wall of Torcross.'

Torcross Point is where the A379 from Kingsbridge makes a south-north hairpin around the southern end of Slapton Ley, on its way to Stoke Fleming and Dartmouth. For those in a hurry, and those who do not want to follow the next 6 miles of the Coast Path, this is the place to catch a Western National 93 bus – there are about ten a day – to Stoke Fleming, Dartmouth or back to Salcombe.

Although Torcross, the village at the southern end of the freshwater lagoon or lake of Slapton Ley, and at the end of Slapton Sands, is a very popular holiday resort in summer, it has changed little as a village. There is a good pub, the Start Bay, and a row of houses, including some fishermen's cottages from the days when the only industry was fishing. Sidney Heath wrote of: '. . . some magnificent Newfoundland dogs that belong to the fishermen, who, when the surf is so rough that the incoming boats cannot approach near enough to cast a rope ashore, send these dogs into the surf, where they pick up the loose ends of the cables and return with them to their masters.' The only dogs I saw when I passed through Torcross were a dachshund and a pair of Sealyhams, none of them quite the build to send into the roaring breakers with encouraging cries of 'Fetch, Rover!'

The next 6 miles have earned much vilification from Coast Path walkers, and bus alternatives have been recommended. In high summer this walk along the Coast Path, a few feet landwards of the A379 and with a narrow stretch of heathy or sedgy land dividing the walker from Slapton Ley, can very often be a muggy slog, with the ears and eyes assaulted by the constant whoosh and exhaust fumes of passing traffic. But I have walked this path in spring when the traffic is reasonably light and the sedgy borders of the Ley are noisy with the excited sounds of courting or nesting birds.

Slapton Ley is more correctly Slapton Leys, since at the southern or Torcross end is Lower Ley, the larger of the two freshwater lakes, and Slapton Ley widens out beyond a broad neck at Hartshorn Plantation. These lakes, separated from the sea by a narrow raised beach of coarse sand and shingle known as Slapton Sands, are fed by two streams, and the water in the Leys drains away through the shingle into the sea. This reef is similar to, but shorter than, the Chesil Beach off the coast of Dorset. The Leys are well-stocked with pike, roach, perch, bass, and rudd. The richness of the water plants, particularly in the nearly overgrown northern part, brings many migrating birds in spring and autumn; waterfowl come to winter there; and in the reedy north there are sedge and reed warblers. Slapton Ley is about two miles long and is a nature reserve, while in Slapton village there is the Slapton Ley Field Study Centre and a bird-watching post of the Devon Bird-watching and Preservation Society. In the spring there are so many bird-watchers that the birds lose all self-consciousness – or maybe play to the ornithological gallery – and I have seen, within a few yards of the road, ducks on the nest and others waddling around surrounded by ducklings. Even if you are not a bird-watcher, it is worth taking along a well-illustrated pocket guide to British birds so that you may recognize what you encounter along the way.

I once walked this path in the middle of the night in early June, and that, too, was rewarding. The waters of the Ley lay like polished steel under the moon and the chugging, clicking, keening, and scolding of the waterfowl made a continuous concert. But you have to keep on the move, because the midges and other insects that thrive thereabouts home in on the even-temporarily stationary traveller. In the daytime in summer the Leyside is yellow with charlock and scarlet with poppies.

For those who make the occasional excursion across the road to walk for a while on the beach, there is, halfway along Slapton Sands, a granite obelisk reminder of recent history – a monument put up by the US Army: '. . . presented to the people of the South Hams who generously left their homes and their lands to provide a battle practice area for the successful assault on Normandy in

June 1944.' Well, yes, in a way. More than 200 farms were evacuated by command, rather than being 'generously left', at the end of 1943 for a year. At least the occupants were thanked and managed to get back to their homes and land, which is more than the Purbeckers got from the British Army. Little thanks and no return for them, as I recount in *The Dorset Coast Path* (see p.171).

At the very northern tip of Slapton Ley a turning to the left over Slapton Bridge leads, in three-quarters of a mile, to Slapton village where, as mentioned earlier, there is a Field Study centre. For those in search of a break, this attractive village has the Tower Inn, taking its name from the tower and walls of the former church house founded by Sir Guy de Brien, Bryan, or Brian in 1372, parts of the walls being incorporated later in a Georgian house called The Priory. The church of St James is early fourteenth-century, and has a splendid Victorian pulpit carved with oaks and pomegranates, and set, goblet-fashion, on a much earlier base.

At the northern end of Slapton Sands the A379 makes a right-angled turn inland but the Coast Path proper is picked up again. Follow the signs, 'To Car Park and Public Conveniences', and about fifty yards up this track there is a gate on the right bearing the acorn sign and a yellow arrow. It is not entirely clear whether one should continue up the track or take the path on the other side of the gate. It is in fact the track, which is the old road, that one takes, above the low cliffs green with elder and brambles. Down on the beach are a couple of winches, one that might just about manage to haul up a boat, and the other a rusty ruin. A number of small boats are usually drawn up on the shingle, through which grow heath, mallow, campion, and foxglove. Pale sloping cliffs mark this part of the coast along to a point called The Slide beyond Pilchard Cove. The vegetation along here, both on the shore and on the upper path, is profuse and colourful, bright with viper's bugloss and yellow sea-poppy. The path veers inland and soon meets the A379 again. Walk along the road for a hundred yards, and look out for a gate on the left; walk up through the field, and take the first gate to the right on to a track that comes out on a road near both Strete church and the Start

Bay Youth Hostel. Turn right and then left, passing the Tallis
Rock Hotel (my perverted sense of humour set me to wondering
if one could score one of Thomas Tallis's anthems as Tudor rock,
just as Benny Goodman wrote 'Mr Bach goes to Town'), and
emerging once more on the A379 which is difficult to get away
from on this stretch of the walk. But also look out in Strete for the
King's Arms which, in addition to its beer and snacks, has a fine
wrought-iron balcony.

   Once on the main road one is faced again with a choice. Either
walk along the road for nearly a mile and visit Blackpool Sands,
or take an unsatisfactory inland route (which the South West Way
Association is trying to improve upon) which keeps one off the
main road until Stoke Fleming. Blackpool Sands is a delightful
little cove having nothing in common with the other place, famed
for Labour Party Conferences and Illuminations, apart from
getting crowded in the summer. There is a car-park, lavatories,
good swimming, and a sheltered position – where, however,
Breton raiders at the beginning of the fifteenth century found no
shelter but were driven out to sea again by the locals. If you do
not go down to Blackpool Sands, watch out for a turning off the
A379 to the left, marked 'Unsuitable for Motor Vehicles', which
has some attractive thatched cottages along it. Less than a quarter
of a mile up this lane there is a stone bridge over the gurgling
stream that runs close by a house of seventeenth- or
eighteenth-century appearance (I have not seen it close to) called
Blackpool Farm. Almost opposite this bridge is a nearly concealed
Public Bridleway signpost, pointing to a stony track between
trees, leading over a hill, alongside a wood on private land, and
coming out on a track where you turn right on a macadam
surface just above Stoke Fleming church. Dating from the
thirteenth to the fifteenth centuries, its tower was used in the past
as a guide to ships entering Dartmouth Harbour. In the nave is
one of the oldest brasses in the country, to John Corp who died in
1351 and to his grand-daughter who died in 1391. John is
portrayed nearly lifesize, his hair parted in the middle and curled
at the ends, his long gown cuffed with fur, a dagger at his belt,
and wearing shoes with very long and pointed toes. His

grand-daughter Eleynore wears a close-fitting gown, and a crenellated headdress with three rose-shaped ornaments in the front and a flying veil. She stands on a pedestal, to make her as tall as her grandfather. This fine brass takes one back in a few seconds to the Middle Ages.

Another memorial, with an inscription and a shield of arms, is in tribute to Elias Newcomen, rector of Stoke Fleming, who died 13 July 1614. His great-grandson was Thomas Newcomen of Dartmouth (1663–1729), inventor of the atmospheric steam engine, who, with two colleagues, thought up a 'fire engine' of greatly improved design, upon which James Watt improved even further. A sadly battered effigy of a woman of around AD 1300 might be that of the wife of Sir John Carew, born Eleanor Mohun of a family to which the manor here belonged, and which is encountered again on the Coast Path at Moonfleet in Dorset.

There is another choice of route here. Either head north up the road opposite the church until you reach a footpath sign, turn right here, and then left, and come out on the A379, which you cross to the lane that goes coastwards from Windward Cottage; or else take the A379 out of Stoke Fleming for half a mile and then turn right at Windward Cottage. But another half-mile north along the A379 there is the Deer Park Holiday Estate (tel: Stoke Fleming 253), where there is a shop and a bar; and if you decide to pitch your tent there among the other tents and caravans, you can have the facilities of launderette, lavatories and showers. I once did that very early in the season, and found it a good place to stock up and sort out the rucksack. A little further up the A379 is Poundhouse and a turning to the right which joins the road leading from Windward Cottage.

By whatever route you come from Windward Cottage (the playing-fields to the left of the road are a good landmark opposite the Windward turning), less than a mile down the lane is a National Trust car-park where there is a signpost directing the walker to the Coast Path, along a fenced route that leads to the clifftop at Warren Cove and along a bracken-lined path that becomes a way between gorse and brambles. There is a welcome bench, just before the Path curves around to the left and stays to the seaward side of a stone wall that has taken over from the earlier barbed-wire fence. There are other wooden benches along this part of the path, set in summer in a forest of foxgloves.

Beyond the Coast Guard hut, which is clapboard set on top of a concrete plinth and looks somewhat like the bridge of a ship, the path is lined by elder and hawthorn, and crosses a narrow stream by a plank bridge, bordered by nettles and bracken, to a stile. It then goes around a deep and chasm-like bay, beyond which is a stile to the left which should be ignored as this is not the Coast Path. In the hedge, and somewhat hidden in the summer, is a Coast Path sign directing you along the Path that closely follows the clifftop, until a point where it begins to drop steeply, bordered by bushes and trees. The Coast Guard lookout is on Combe Point, and the rocks off the coast are called Inner Combe and Outer Combe Rocks. Beyond Combe Point is steep-sided Shiglehill Cove. Rounding a slight cape, the Path leads to Willow Cove, and after a more curving cape there is the deep indentation of Compass Cove, above which is a long white building called Cable House, its original purpose advertised by great, wooden, diamond-shaped boards, somewhat battered by wind and weather, lettered 'Telegraph Cable'.

At the point where the Coast Path passes below Cable House, there is a path interspersed with some battered steps going down to Compass Cove between its steeply wooded sides. One morning very early I went down there, watched beadily by seagulls on their nests, and had a swim in what turned out to be a kind of chilled seaweed minestrone. Bits of green weed stuck to my legs, and that night I found that I was still iodine-scented and streaked like Derby sage cheese.

At one time there must have been some kind of building in this cove, because there are torn-down concrete steps set on their sides by the sea, and great cables swoop out of the cliffs and dive under the sand. It is a slight detour to the shore but when the weather is good, and if the sea is not too solid with seaweed, it is worth it. The steep sides of this secluded cove are white with ox-eye daisies, and mauve with sea-cabbage.

Back on the Path, the way goes down gradually, with a view of the sea-lashed rocks on the shore and bracken and gorse on both sides, until a sudden dip is negotiated by steps cut into the earth and shored up by planks. At the foot of the steps is a smart blue-and-white painted bench, set beside a ravine-like inlet crossed by a railed plank bridge. The rocks on the seaward side hold pools of water and are covered with thrift growing almost to the edge of the sea. The chasm ends in a narrow cave in the cliffs, framed by marguerites and foxgloves.

Further along the Path there is a much-vandalized lookout hut with mast and spars. Here the Path becomes rocky and begins to climb again, until it is overhung by plane trees with high banks of bracken to the left. The white bladder campion gives way to willowherb, buttercups, cow parsley, and a lot of ivy which, where it has brought down the trees on which it had climbed, carries on interlacing across the fallen trunks. When the trees are in leaf the

Castle Ferry, Dartmouth

sea is almost out of sight, and the Path is a green tunnel noisy with blackbirds, thrushes, wood pigeons, and the seabirds further down the green cliffs.

The trees on the landward side become much taller – plane, ash, chestnut, occasional sallow – and on the right are some houses sheltered from the path by a hawthorn hedge. At the end of the path there is a flight of steps leading to a totally concealed house called 'Wavendon', which has a garden bright in summer with lupins, sweet williams, and marigolds. From this point the track becomes a tarmac drive and comes out on a narrow road at Compass Cottage, still in a tunnel of shade between oaks and beeches where a wall holds up the hillside – a stone wall speckled blue, white, and yellow with ivy-leaved toadflax. A notice points the way from which we have come as 'To Compass Hill and

The Dart Estuary

Compass Cove', and to the left there is a lower path leading to
Sugary Cove. Immediately opposite, on the rising landward side
there is a National Trust sign leading to Gallants' Bower. Carry
on down this tarmac road: it leads to a jetty from which, in
summer, there is a ferry up to the centre of Dartmouth and the
point where the Lower Ferry crosses to Kingswear.

10 Dartmouth

A road above and running to the right of the Castle Ferry leads to
the Castle, which guards this narrowest part of the Dart Estuary
in conjunction with Kingswear Castle across the river. Norman on
Saxon stone foundations and much of it now under the ground,
the surviving square tower was raised in the reign of Edward IV
and the round tower was built in the reign of Henry VII.
Travellers to the Crusades sailed from Dartmouth in 1147 and
1190, and so did the Pilgrim Fathers in 1620, in *Speedwell* and
Mayflower. In the intervening centuries the town grew in
importance, size and wealth through the wine trade with France.
Chaucer, as Inspector of Customs, visited Dartmouth in 1373 and
wrote in the Prologue to the *Canterbury Tales*:

> A shipman was ther, wonynge fer by weste;
> For aught I woot, he was of Dertemouthe. . . .
> Ful many a draughte of wyn had he ydrawe
> From Burdeux-ward, whil that the chapman sleep.
> Of nyce conscience took he no keep.
> If that he faught, and hadde the hyer hand,
> By water he sente him hoom to every lond.

Chaucer's shipman may have been based on Sir John Hawley, a
rich and powerful shipowner and merchant who was seven times
Mayor of Dartmouth, owning so many ships that it was said: 'Blow
the wind high, blow the wind low, It bloweth good to Hawley's
hoe' – i.e., to the high point in the harbour where Hawley's quay
and warehouses lay.

Dartmouth Castle, on whose ramparts a reconditioned cannon
stands at a point where one can get a good idea of the castle's

Dartmouth Castle

strategic importance, was originally built by Hawley in 1388 as a
defence against Breton raiders. A chain guarded the Dart estuary
at this point, the other end being secured to a tower of Kingswear
Castle, and in the Second World War this protection was renewed
by steel cable, nets and wooden floats to keep out German
submarines.

In the summer there is a small teashop open at the castle, and
the mind too can be refreshed in St Petroc's Church's simple
whitewashed interior. It was founded 1400 years ago by the saint
as a wooden shrine; look at its present-day ceiling decorated with
suns and stars, most appropriate for a church that has seen so
many ships sailing out to sea, and at the memorials and brasses,
some a reminder of how much shorter life used to be than it is
now. Barbara Plumleigh 'dyed when age had neere run out, ye

Four and XXXth yeare'. She had borne two sons and four daughters, and is depicted as having been 'a neighbour kinde, In all distresse a tender-harted frende'. Age comes up again, where John Roope is shown as a young man of pleasing appearance, with a note of surprise: "Twas not a winded nor a withred face'.

Winded and withered or not, the traveller should take some time off from the Path to visit Dartmouth, one of the most delightful small towns in England. It is romantic, picturesque, packed with history from before the Crusades; through the times when Sir Walter Ralegh's *Roebuck* brought in *Madre de Dios*, a prize of prodigious riches; to the building, 1899–1905, of the orange and white Dartmouth Naval College that stands high over the town; and the sailing of US soldiers to the Norman beaches in 1944. And all around are ancient buildings, like the overhanging gables supported by eleven carved stone pillars along the Butterwalk in Duke Street; and St Saviour's Church, mainly of the fourteenth century, with its great screen that still retains traces of the original colours, and its carved stone pulpit. In the brass to John Hawley and his two wives, he is depicted as a knight in plate armour, and not as a Member of Parliament and merchant. In this church in 1663 Thomas Newcomen was baptized and later gave his name to a Dartmouth street. There is a memorial in the public gardens to this man who was 'the first to conceive the idea of working a piston by steam', and the Newcomen Society re-erected in 1964 one of Newcomen's engines which had been built in 1725 and was altered in 1821. Would all readers named Watt kindly write to the Newcomen Society and not to Messrs Constable or to me.

11 Dartmouth to Brixham

Dartmouth Lower Ferry operates throughout the year, seven days a week, starting at 0700 (0800 Sundays), last departure 2215. On leaving the ferry at Kingswear, turn right on the other side of the road and pass under an archway to Alma Steps, which climb up to Beacon Road. Turn right along Beacon Road, which becomes a narrow track between walled gardens and houses, and continue above Kingswear Castle and Mill Bay Cove, where the

Path turns north – an unsatisfactory but, it is hoped, temporary official path running inland until it rejoins the coast 3½ miles on at Man Sands. From Mill Bay Cove a pleasant narrow road leads to Home Farm where there is a sharp turn to the right over a little bridge, leading directly into a rocky track that climbs steadily through trees. The rocks are very slippery when it is wet, as I found out when I plunged forward, camera at the ready, into the mud. At the top of the hill, a cottage is well-named Rocky Lane Cottage.

The road becomes tarmac soon after the top, and has farm buildings on the right, and on the left a massive wall enclosing the garden of a big house which is Brownstone Farm. The road continues to climb gently past beehives on the left; over to the right can be seen the 80-ft limestone tower raised in 1864 as a Day Mark, first glimpsed from the other side of the estuary on the approach to Dartmouth. Closer to, it looks smaller than from a few miles off, not much more than an overgrown triangulation point, in fact. Cottages on the left are called New Cottages, but do not look it, and further on there are high banks on both sides of the track, with on the crest of the hill three Scots pines and a large metal water-tank on the left. There is a gate here and on the other side of it a stern notice: 'Private Drive, no vehicles except on farm business, public footpath to Kingswear, no access to the sea.' A little further on, a gateway on the right is marked clearly as a private farm road, and another notice tells us that we have just come from Brownstone Farm. I am in favour of such clear signposting and information about where the right of way lies and where it does not.

This tarmac track comes out on to a broader public road with a house on the right. Carry straight on, leaving Kingston Farm on the left, and at a fork in the road take the right-hand one marked 'To Woodhuish Farm'. This is Scabbacombe Lane, a roughish track going down sharply to Man Sands, a small bay just beyond Crabrock Point. There are some former Coast Guard cottages here, and close to the shore a limekiln where Berry Head limestone was brought by sea to be burned for use as fertilizer. Man Sands are not sand, but fine grey and mauve shingle.

There is a stiff climb to the top of Southdown Cliff (350 ft) on

good springy turf and to the inside of a wire fence. This is the
Southdown National Trust area. Further along there is still the
wire fence to the left, and to the right a hawthorn hedge hiding
the sea. The flourishing vegetation in the undercliff includes ash,
elder, plane, hazel, and what I hope was a young elm. The Path
carries on over rounded clifftops covered with bramble and
bracken, and just above Sharkham Point there is a solid new stile
with the National Trust sign beside it to show the limit of the
Southdown area. From this point the Path begins to go downhill,
following the curve inland of St Mary's Bay, and then opens into a
broad and well-trodden path around Durl Head and past a
holiday camp, where it takes the seaward side of the fence to
come out on the track at the Berry Head promontory.

At Berry Head in summer there is a packed car-park, and even
in winter it is only worth walking around the perimeter of the
Head if you wish to examine the hummocks of the Iron Age
cliff-fort, or the fortifications raised against the French at the

The Coast Path rounds Sharkham Point

time of the wars against Bonaparte. The whole of Berry Head is a
common, in fact a grassy plateau Country Park which in early
spring is a breeding-ground for razorbills, kittiwakes, fulmars,
and herring gulls. The Head has a great glassy mushroom
air-navigation beacon, with a clearly marked path around it
running down between trees, by a sloping path with steps here
and there, to a road beside a massive brick tower which was a
fuel-storage point during the Second World War. An alternative
is to take the road marked 'No Entry' immediately opposite the
entrance to the Berry Head car-park, down to the same brick
tower and the Berry Head Hotel immediately ahead. Turn left at
the end of this road and you are on the main seafront road
leading into Brixham, with rows of guest-houses and hotels on
the left and the shore on the right with, now and then, glimpses of
the 1,000-yard-long Victoria Breakwater that protects an
anchorage of 140 acres.

12 Brixham to the Teign

Although Brixham is no longer the small fishing village which it
used to be, and it has been afflicted by the dread, incurable
British disease of seaside sprawl, there is an old centre of narrow
streets which gives an idea of the past. Or there is the 117 bus
from Berry Head Road to Fishcombe Road, where the Path is
found again, leading through woods to Churston Cove, where it
then runs on the seaward side of the fence around Churston Golf
Course. Keep inland of the trees to Elberry Cove, and then carry
on along the clifftop around Churston Point to Broad Sands. As
the Path is not very clearly defined, it is as well to remember to
stay inside the line of trees and not be led on to any of the many
paths that run down to the sea on one side and inland on the
other. At Broad Sands the Path comes down to sea level and
crosses a small bridge, where there are public lavatories and a
car-park. Walk along the beach at Broad Sands which has a
curving pebbled bay; from there on, the Path runs parallel to the
landward side of the railway.

While I was reading a Great Western Railway notice with
nostalgia, I heard the sound of a steam engine and along came a

Steam rules between Dartmouth and Torbay!

locomotive hauling a train in the GWR chocolate-and-cream livery. There are two trains in the morning and two in the afternoon throughout the summer and at Christmas: a wonderful piece of living, puffing-and-whistling history.

There is really no reason for the most orthodox stickler to plod every inch through Paignton. I once walked the whole way, regretted it, went visitor-native, ate Cornish soft ice-cream, and only just resisted buying a T-shirt printed with 'Torbay University'. The Coast Path finishes officially at Goodrington Sands, and the best thing to do is get aboard a Western National 122 bus, or, in May and June, the 124, on the A379. In any case, find the nearest bus stop and get on whatever will take you to the other side of Babbacombe, thus avoiding more than 10 miles of British urbanized seaside. The walk is just not worth it.

The official Path begins again at Hope's Nose before Babbacombe. Since I walked there, a path called the Rock End Path has been opened between Petit Tor Cove and Daddyhole Plain. Not having walked it, I cannot comment on it, but it obviously would improve the urban route quite a lot.

At Babbacombe, make your way towards the beach and the pier and you will find the Coast Path starting again just above beach level. It comes out at the eastern end of the car-park and takes advantage of an ordinary footpath with a number of steps along its course, rounding a slight bay with trees above it on the landward side, and leading to the foot of the 1926 cliff railway at Oddicombe. This railway looks rather like the one that clanks up to the Sacré Coeur from the lower slopes of Montmartre. The Path dodges under the railway and goes slightly inland after Oddicombe, passing frequently through trees and on the landward side of well wooded clifftops. At Watcombe Head there is a public lavatory, and the Path stays half-way up the slopes until it reaches a narrow road going down from the main road to a car-park at Maidencombe. Follow this road to a Coast Path sign on the right, which directs you into a road which, when I was last there, was being made up with great chunks of tarmac flayed from some other road, complete with tattoo-marks of single and double yellow no-parking lines. It is some fifty yards long, but watch the other end, at a fork, and be sure to take the right-hand road through a farm gate, leading into a car-park on the far side of which is the Coast Path sign. From here it is 3¼ miles to Teignmouth, along an ordinary footpath through fields, with a thick hedge and trees along the clifftop effectively hiding the sea. In the thickly-populated Torbay area, this section of the Path runs through surprisingly deserted countryside for nearly two miles until, after a steep climb above Labrador Bay, it joins the A379 road. This has to be followed (accompanied by heavy traffic and exhaust fumes in the summer) for about a quarter of a mile, until a stile is reached by a Coast Path signpost to a path over fields sloping down to a grove of oaks, just before it comes out at Shaldon car-park. On the right of the car-park there is a tunnel through red rock cliffs to Ness Beach. The walls of the tunnel are

The Oddicombe funicular

as red as the rock through which it passes, although the tunnel-lining is made of stone blocks, probably the same stone as the cliff itself. It is one of the spookiest tunnels I have ever been in, dimly lit, echo-haunted, smelling of damp and carrying the sound of the sea from its other end – sea which occasionally comes into the tunnel at high tide. But if it is the right time of day, season, and tide, there is swimming at Ness Beach.

Beyond the car-park there are public gardens with a good view over Shaldon, and beach huts on a spit of sand. The ferry to Teignmouth leaves at about twenty-minute intervals, starting at 0800 hrs throughout the year and ending at times varying between 1700 and 2200 according to season (tel: Teignbridge District Council, Tourism Department, Teignmouth 6271, or consult the *South West Way: a Complete Guide*, ferry section).

Should you arrive when the ferry is not in operation, it is only a
half-mile walk into Shaldon to the bridge across to Teignmouth, a
town of 12,000 inhabitants set on the estuary of the River Teign
which rises on Dartmoor. It is a town with a thousand years of
history and a seal dating back to that unfortunate, but
ever-remembered, monarch Ethelred the Unready. There is little
left of the town's remote past, and not too much of its blossoming
as the 'fashionable watering-place' which it was in 1803. Some
careful searching is needed to find Regency and early Victorian
architecture. The quay was built in 1821 to facilitate the shipping
of Dartmoor granite to London to rebuild London Bridge, now
bereft of Thames damp and parching in a United States desert.
Teignmouth is cheerful, bright with gardens, has a flamboyant
Den Crescent of 1826, a most Royal Hotel, and a lighthouse of
pocket proportions which has stood at the end of the promenade
since 1845.

13 The Teign to the Exe

There is not much to recommend the 9 miles from Teignmouth
to Starcross which can be covered in several ways, most of them
pretty dull. After leaving the ferry from Shaldon on the
Teignmouth side, there is no official Coast Path for the next 4
miles. There is a bus route, the 186/187, to Dawlish where the
Path may be picked up again, or there is a route that can be
walked. Go up the road to the fork if you want to take the bus
along the A379, but if you choose to walk, check on the tide first,
for at low tide it is possible to walk along the beach. Except in
gale-force winds or at high tide, you can also walk along the sea
wall, with the beach on one side and the main Paddington to
Penzance railway-line on the other. If you choose the latter, take
the tunnel – which you cannot do at high tide – under the railway,
up Smugglers' Lane to Holcombe where there are buses, a post
office and shops. From Holcombe to beyond Dawlish there is no
official Coast Path and it is as well to catch a bus to the other side
of Dawlish because the main road along which you have to walk is
hell in summer and lorry-splashed in winter.

As you approach Dawlish there is a footbridge, opposite the

Roman Catholic church, which crosses the omnipresent railway and leads down to the shore. This can also be reached by going into Dawlish itself and turning seawards from the square beyond the station, and so on to the promenade. Unfortunately the railway, Brunel's formidable construction, and the tunnels through the red sandstone, dominate the seafront at Dawlish. The little town is well laid out, and the Daw waterfalls through it on its way to the sea. Dawlish is the setting for the opening of *Nicholas Nickleby*, too heavy a book to carry for Pathside reading.

When the tide is out, there is a walk on the sands, to seaward of the shore-hugging railway, until Langstone Rock has been passed, and then there is a tunnel under the railway just before Dawlish Warren station. The village is built on a sandspit that sticks out like a thick beckoning finger across three-quarters of the estuary of the River Exe. There is a caravan site, a golf-course, and a nature reserve, but nothing will take the Coast Path walker anywhere except to a tantalizing view of Exmouth across the water.

To get to Exmouth, you have to walk along the road to Starcross where there is the choice of taking the ferry straight to Exmouth (seven sailings per day during the summer; for times tel: Exmouth 72009); of taking a bus to Exeter and another down to Exmouth; or taking a train from Dawlish Warren station to Exeter and changing there for a train to Exmouth.

At a demi-loop in the road from Dawlish Warren to Starcross there is a hamlet called Cockwood (coyly pronounced Co'wood) that has a most pleasant pub, the Anchor, outside which in good weather one may sit and watch the railway persisting on its seemingly precarious way across the sands. My feeling is that it is better merely to watch the train but to take the bus from the Anchor, because the chances are that you will get around to Exmouth in less time.

At Starcross there is a unique slice of industrial history to be studied and savoured. Isambard Brunel had worked out a plan for driving a train between Exeter and Plymouth by atmospheric pressure on a piston attached to the train, the pressure to one side and a vacuum on the other being contained in a continuous pipe

sealed with leather flaps and running between the lines. It did not
work. A memorial to the idea still stands in an Italianate red
sandstone building in Starcross that was one of the original
pumping stations, and in the name of the 'Atmospheric Railway'
pub. Pressurized beer aside, I bet there is not another pub in the
world with that name.

14 The Exe to the Otter

Exmouth sits on a spit of land at the estuary of the River Exe
which rises on Exmoor in Somerset and makes its way here
through Tiverton and Exeter. It was anciently a port, ravaged by
the Danes in AD 1003, and it supplied 10 ships and nearly 200
men for Edward III's expedition to Calais in 1347. The town now
consists of remnants of what was built in the early eighteenth
century when it began to be popular, because of its long sandy
beach, as a watering place for Exeter families, together with rows
of small houses built in Victorian times and after.

Turn right on leaving the quay where (it is hoped) you have
landed from the ferry. The Coast Path takes you along the
Esplanade and its continuation, Marine Drive. Make time to turn
off the Esplanade and walk into the town up Bath Road to the
Beacon, a modest rise where a street of Georgian houses was built
at the end of the eighteenth century when Exmouth was enjoying
its fashionable success. At No 6, a Georgian red-brick house, lived
Frances, Lady Nelson where she saw more of the sea than she did
of her husband. At No 5, an Italianate villa, lived Anne Isabella,
Lady Byron, also in a state of grass-widowhood *trompée*. Holy
Trinity Church, completed in 1824, is of amazing proportions for
a parish church of a place the size of Exmouth at that time. It was
altered and made even larger at the beginning of the twentieth
century, and in sheer bulk remains imposing.

In summer, the walk along the Esplanade, when one is dressed
in boots, carrying a rucksack, tent and the rest, draws looks from
open-shirted or flowery-dressed holidaymakers, and gives one
the feeling of being in a space-suit. The Esplanade and Marine
Drive, and the curve of sandy beach to the red cliffs at the eastern
end, all lie in a span of two miles. At the end of the town is a

Lifeboat House and Lifeboat Museum which has a fine collection of photographs of rescues, lifeboats, and crews of the past. The beach huts, varied in slight and cunning ways, stand side by side like soldiers on parade at the edge of the sea. One that took my fancy had a wrought-iron name on it – 'OSOKOZE'. In a large pool of seawater left by the tide were three tripper swans from the Exe Estuary who were being photographed and fed, no doubt following a familiar busking routine which on that day looked profitable in terms of bread and buns. At the end of Marine Drive there is a vast car-park, set against the red Orcombe cliffs, and the Orcombe Café. You can either take the path that leads up from the car-park, or carry on right to the end of the promenade (or along the beach at low tide) and then climb the steps to the heathy clifftop area called the Maer. Through this runs the Path to

'Osokoze' – a beach hut at Exmouth

A friend at Sandy Bay

Budleigh Salterton, soon opening out into a field where one must
ignore all stiles on the left leading inland into other broad fields.

The High Land of Orcombe is National Trust property and is
called High Land for the good reason that it is on top of a 250-ft
high red sandstone cliff. This is good open going on firm turf,
with a low line of brambles on the seaward side of the path. There
are few trees, and a fine view of Straight Point jutting into the sea,
but this cannot be explored because the whole of the peninsula is
a closely fenced rifle-range. Sandy Bay earns its name because, as
I saw when I was there and the tide was out, there is an expanse of
sand with shingle at the foot of the red cliffs. Out beyond Straight
Point I saw a long curving swathe of water which was of a
different colour, almost as though it might be freshwater, but
there is no estuary here and it must reflect the curve on the other

side of the Point.

The Path begins to drop gently from the top of the cliff as the giant Sandy Bay caravan site comes into view. There is an equally giant car-park, where a wall spreads the riveting news that 'Birmingham City rules the Midlands OK?' The Path stays close to the outside of the rifle range's tall wire fence, on the other side of which, fearing nothing but small-arms fire and military desolation, were seven donkeys and a piebald pony. The donkeys stood and gave me considered looks, but the pony came to the fence and took a few raisins between his piano-key teeth – which had often negotiated that wire if dental dexterity was anything to go by. Just beyond here is a pleasant little landscaped park or garden, carefully and thoughtfully planted with rock plants, cistus and stocks, with a palm tree here and there, and many garden seats in sheltered positions. Beyond the last of the caravans a Coast Path sign shows that the Path goes off to the left, with another path leading down to Otter Cove.

A stile beyond the caravan park, and I was in a different world. Looking over Littleham Cove to Budleigh Bay, there are red cliffs, and grey and pink pebbles on the beach; and on the top of the cliff over which the Path goes, I saw fields being ploughed, the red earth turning up dustily behind the tractor with its attendant pennant of seagulls. In this rolling land, beyond and sometimes below the clifftop line are little copses and plantations with the by-now-familiar sad lone shapes of dead elms. There was the drifting smoke and warm smell of a weed fire, and the shades of red of this Devon soil, varying according to how recently it had been turned and worked. Beyond this field, steps lead down to a stile and a little wooden bridge between oak and alder, where there is not much evidence of the stream that flows below. Beyond the bridge a flight of well made and well preserved wooden steps leads to a short path that runs out to the edge of the cliff, but the Coast Path goes straight ahead up the side of the next field. When I turned and looked back, I saw that those dead elms were being felled by a power saw and hauled away by the tractor that had just been ploughing. Its rear wheels threw up great clouds of red dust as they slipped in the dry soil. This rural

scene was suddenly shattered by the noise of firing on the
rifle-range – perhaps a mass execution of tourists to accompany
the toppling elms?

There is a stiffish climb to the top of West Down Beacon, where
a green-painted seat faces west towards a magnificent view. This
gorse-covered down is charred in patches, more by accident than
by some clearing design, and below and around the gorse are
ground-creeping brambles and heather. Along this stretch of
coast there is a wild undercliff, thickly covered with a jungle of
bramble, gorse, and stunted hawthorn, called The Floors; it
extends for two miles from Littleham Cove nearly to Budleigh
Salterton.

At the triangulation point on top of West Down is another
welcome green, park-style bench by the fence, and on the other
side of the fence is a golf-course. As I sat there for a drink and a
breather, I saw two women playing golf with enthusiasm and
energetic enjoyment. One wore a skirt of a shade that used to be
called electric blue, and the other a green skirt to narrow the eyes
and bring out the Irish. Between strokes these two bronzed and
happy tropical-coloured birds shared a white cup of something
refreshing – lemonade, tea, dry martini? If only I had had a
colour film in my camera at that moment!

The path leads into woods just beyond the golf-course, woods
of pine, dwarf holly, and what looked like feral fruit trees, bullace
or wild plum perhaps. There is something of a wilderness along
here, with gorse, bracken, and more and more holly, until the
path comes out into a lane leading off left into the west end of the
seafront at Budleigh Salterton, which is the Coast Path route.

The River Otter rises in the Somerset Blackdown Hills and
flows southward through the Honiton Valley. Its name is present
in Ottery St Mary – where Samuel Taylor Coleridge was born in
1772 when his father was vicar there – in Ottery Venn, and in
Otterton just east of Budleigh Salterton. At one time, but
probably not since the end of the fifteenth century, this estuary
was used as a harbour; but by the time Leland came to write of it
in his *Itinerary* (1540) he recorded that less than 100 ships used
the haven, because it had silted up. Some of the land at the mouth

was reclaimed in the early nineteenth century, which made it even more difficult to enter the river. On the estuary salt-making was carried on for centuries, certainly from Saxon times and down to the eighteenth century, and it is from the 'salterns', Anglo-Saxon *Sealter-tun* – 'place of the salters'? – that the second part of the town's name is derived.

Budleigh Salterton now is a small, pleasant town, surrounded by pine and beech woods and built for the most part along and off one long main street. Architecturally, it is both pleasing and unremarkable, consisting mostly of comfortable villas built in the early years of this century, with gardens facing the sea, together with a red-brick Georgian terrace, and some pretty Victorian cottages in, naturally, Victoria Place. On the steeply shelving beach Sir John Millais painted his 'Boyhood of Raleigh', exhibited

Hayes Barton near Budleigh Salterton, where Sir Walter Ralegh was born in 1552

at the Royal Academy in 1870 and one of the most frequently reproduced and most familiar Victorian paintings. Ralegh (perhaps the preferable spelling) was born around 1552 at Hayes Barton, just over a mile to the north-west, now a farmhouse. In 1584 he tried to buy 'hayes a farme som tyme in my fathers possession . . . being borne in that howse I had rather seat my sealf ther than any wher els'. But although he was powerful at Court at the time, he did not succeed in buying Hayes Barton.

In All Saints Church at East Budleigh there are 63 carved bench ends, varying from the head of an American Indian to the Ralegh coat of arms. It is worth visiting Hayes Barton and East Budleigh, but it does mean a diversion of about two miles from the Coast Path, which has hereabouts a diversion of its own.

The provision of a bridge at the mouth of the Otter has been under discussion for many years and is constantly raised by the South West Way Association with both the Countryside Commission and the Devon County Council. At present the diversion is by way of a footpath leading inland from the car-park at the eastern end of the Promenade. Take the turning to the left just before the car-park, and a few yards along is a lane to the right; immediately inside the lane is a stile on the left to a clearly marked footpath leading along reed-bordered tributaries of the Otter with, on the left, high rocky banks topped by gardens, and overhanging trees dripping with old man's beard. Obviously you take the first bridge, White Bridge, over the Otter and this is about 1½ miles upstream. Over the bridge there is a road to South Farm, with South Farm cottages immediately in front of you. Go through the gate, cross the cattle-grid to a Coast Path sign directing you along the left of a wood high on the bank of the Otter, with some Scots pines at the top. Down below, a line of willows and poplars near the water shows the edge of the very marshy Otter estuary. As you approach the cliff, which slopes here back inland, watch out carefully for the path and do not go to the very tip of the point above the estuary.

Two alternatives to this inland detour will at once occur to all but the most unadventurous of Coast Path walkers (are there any?). Nobody is ever content to merely follow instructions and

South Farm, close to the point where the Otter is crossed

turn left like an obedient soldier at the end of Budleigh Salterton Promenade. One just has to go and look at the tumble of rocks called Otterton Edge beyond the estuary. Once there, it is obviously easy to cross at low tide to the farther bank, where we all want to get to when travelling eastwards. BUT, a deep channel at the foot of sheer cliffs cuts you off from getting inland, and you can neither climb the cliffs from further east along the beach nor get round what is rightly marked on the map as Danger Point. Abandon any idea of reaching the eastward-going Coast Path from the seaward side.

There is an alternative, which must be treated with cautious respect. This is to wade the mouth of the Otter, as I did once in calm and dry weather, and at low tide. Find the narrowest point, which is below the reedy marshes; on the west side it consists of

banks of shingle and rocks, and on the east side of a dark red
vertical cliff with, at low tide, enough visible shingle at its foot to
let you get around to the left, keeping close to the rock face, until
you get to where it opens out inland. You can then climb up to the
top of the wood and find the Coast Path. I tied my boots, socks,
and trousers to the top of my rucksack and, without being more
than waist-deep, I crossed the ten or twelve yards to the other
side. The water was too cloudy to see where I was setting my feet,
but the feel was of hard shingle – no mud, weed, rocks, or rusty
cans, nor any current to speak of. But after rain it is, I am sure, a
hazardous crossing that should not be attempted. Anyway the
inland detour is a very pleasant one.

15 The Otter to the Sid

Once across the Otter, by whatever route, and having found the
Coast Path which does not start at the very point of the estuary
cliff but joins the clifftop just above Danger Point, stay close to the
edge of the cliffs that drop sheer to the sea – a fence prevents
walkers from doing the same. Inland lie pasture and cultivated
fields. It is very pleasant walking with little evidence, apart from a
tractor or a few cows, that any human beings live around here.
Coal Bench and Black Head further on probably commemorate
some shipwreck, as does Brandy Head beyond them – unless it
was named for a seizure of contraband, or for a hangover. There
is access to Poolness Beach, sheltered by Brandy Head and facing
south-west. Just beyond Brandy Head, Twopenny Loaf Rock is
shown on the map but I could see nothing that suggested a penny
roll, a croissant or even a sandwich. A ledge of rocks below the
cliffs is called Crab Ledge – no prize for guessing origins there.
The path hugs the clifftop along the gently curving Chiselbury
Bay, and then takes a sharp left turn inland, crossing a stream by
a footbridge before Ladram Bay Holiday Camp, which is set at
the side of a wooded combe leading down to Ladram Bay, one of
the loveliest spots on the South Devon coast. The Holiday Camp,
caravans, café, and lavatories have been placed so that they are
not visible from the bay itself, which remains much as it must have
been for centuries, with sea-bitten columns of red sandstone

The east bank of the Otter estuary

rising from the water. The beach is sandy and there is excellent swimming from it, or from the sandstone slabs at the western end of the bay. A road comes down to the head of the combe, and for those looking for a break it is only a mile into Otterton.

If you have been down to the beach (which is likely unless there is thick fog or it is pouring with rain), walk up the track into the combe and look out for a blue-and-white painted thatched cottage on the right. Close to it is the Coast Path sign. The Path rises through cultivated land, past a pub called the Three Rocks (open in summer), and then climbs steeply into the Forestry Commission High Peak conifer plantations. The top, 514 ft, has a trig point: I went up there out of curiosity, but it is a pretty thorny detour, and the Path proper is along the fire-break that skirts around the earthworks of a prehistoric cliff-fort.

The Path continues along the saddle called Windgate and then climbs again to gorse-dotted Peak Hill, on top of which is an electric sub-station within its wire compound: just beyond that is a kissing-gate where there is a Coast Path sign pointing down, through high gorse. The view ahead and below opens out and shows the contrasts in colours – the dark red cliffs and the white and pastel colours of the houses in Sidmouth. The path narrows again between more gorse and brambles, with sycamore, plane, and ash trees. Then the gorse gives way altogether, and the path leads between close-packed tall beech trees, coming up against a fence where it turns sharp left towards the road. As you come down the bank on to the road, you can look up at the cast-iron sign that states 'Public Foot . . . Lad . . .', 'path' and 'ram' having been smashed off. (When travelling *westwards*, keep an eye open

Looking east, down to Sidmouth

for these steps up the bank and into the trees, because on the other side all there is to be seen is '. . . oot Path to . . . Bay, 2 miles'. It seemed more than two miles to me.)

The road drops steeply, with houses and their gardens between it and the edge of the cliffs. At a bend in the road is the start of a wide and pleasant greensward leading down to the western end of Sidmouth Esplanade. This is much better walking than continuing down a rather suburban road, and there are benches along the way, particularly convenient when climbing westwards. I was travelling eastwards, and, as it was still fairly early in the morning, there was mist in the distance, but I had a clear view of the way beyond Sidmouth: an up-and-down path, to the seaward of which I could count five headlands. There were probably more to be seen in clear weather.

After the greensward is the Surf Life-Saving Club, and a walled public garden that was bright with marigolds, petunias, fuschias, hydrangeas, asters, lavender, and rock plants, set under some gallant palm trees. A gateway through the high stone wall leads on to a paved clifftop walk. Everywhere there are benches set out of the wind and to catch the sun. These Connaught Gardens 'are intended for rest and quiet. Visitors are asked not to picnic and keep dogs under control.' I tried to work out the grammar of that request, found the gate at the end of the gardens locked, and so came out on to the road again. The Victoria Hotel lives up to its name, red-brick and a white mast from which flutters the Union Jack. On the right of the road, villas, mostly of the 1820s and quite large, have diamond-paned windows and some of them are thatched. Further along is another opulent hotel, the Belmont, all white paint and green verandahs, and approached between two massive stone pillars.

Sidmouth lies in the valley of the little River Sid, with sheltering cliffs on either side. In the Middle Ages there was a harbour, protected by the headland of Chit Rock, but storm and tide brought it into decay and Sidmouth, a borough and market town in the thirteenth century, declined until the popularity of seabathing brought sheltered resorts into favour.

On Christmas Eve, 1819, the ailing Duke of Kent and his wife and infant daughter, Princess Victoria, moved into Woolbrook Cottage on the slopes of Peak Hill. Kent was not only in poor health but he was hard up too, and it was thought that a stay in South Devon would be both beneficial and economical. But a month later, on 23 January 1820, he died, and his widow and Princess Victoria, now heir to the throne, returned to London. In 1866 Queen Victoria presented the west window to the new church as a memorial to her father.

Sidmouth grew swiftly between about 1800 and 1837. Was the Esplanade, built in 1837, a sign of civic pride in the young Princess Victoria, Queen at seventeen? Coming from the wilder west, one of the first buildings encountered on the Esplanade is the Tourist Information Office, open Monday–Friday 1000–1300 and 1400–1700, and on Saturday between 1000 and 1300. There you can get directions to what was Woolbrook Cottage and is now the Royal Glen Hotel, to the splendidly Gothick Beach House on the Esplanade, to the Gothick composition of Coburg Terrace and the rather more formal Georgian Fortfield Terrace. But find time for Sidmouth if you have a taste and eye for English architecture in full early nineteenth-century bloom.

There is a lot of everything in Sidmouth. Just beyond the Tourist Information Office is a first-aid post, and shelters face the sea, so that even if you have a cold you can treat it with sunshine and fresh air. There has to be an Hotel Riviera somewhere, I thought, and there is one – painted white and grey, very elegant, with lots of baby palm trees to bolster the choice of name. The houses in Sidmouth are a cheerful sight, pink, blue, white, grey, and pigeon-coloured. It is all very gay in a muted English way, with none of the more adventurous architecture and colours of the Mediterranean Riviera.

16 Sidmouth to Seaton

The Esplanade and the road both end at the River Sid, over which there is a footbridge followed by a flight of steps. At the top is a post that looks as if it once carried the Coast Path sign, and a plaque stating that here is a nature reserve. Iron railings on the left and wooden railings on the right keep the walker a safe distance from the cliff edge, which is thick with convolvulus, charlock and sheep's parsley. The path is paved up to the point where there begins a very stiff climb, with cultivated fields on the left. The sea to the right is obscured, except for a gap here and there, by tall blackthorn, elder and plane trees. Yarrow and lilac-coloured mallow, toadflax, and patches of presumably self-sown Michaelmas daisies, flourish. Seats have been placed on the steep way up here, either by those whose names are on them, or to commemorate others. The path becomes even steeper, and steps have been cut in the hillside. At the top there is the yellow acorn sign, and the Coast Path climbs on between plane trees. At the very top are more seats with plaques on them; and below, in the valley of the Sid, is the considerable spread of Sidmouth, seeming much larger than when one walked through the town.

The Path comes out into the open, with bracken all around and a kissing-gate on the right, and again the acorn sign to prove that one is still on the right track. On the other side of a gate is a big slab of granite, chamfered at the top, which, although it has lost a few letters, is still clearly inscribed: 'Southcombe Farm, including the hill summit of Salcombe Hill, dedicated by the owner as a permanent open space, Vaughan Cornish, 1937', followed by: 'No sounds of worldly toil ascending there, admire the full in burst of prayer.' This is an open, grassy space and you must keep to the seaward side across the fields to an iron farm gate. Beyond this gate there is a block of stone in a kind of amalgam of flint, somewhat unexpected here, and a little further on a limestone marker has the word 'path' cut, and marked with black arrows to show both east and west.

There is a very steep descent of Dunscombe Cliff where the Path has been worn smooth, and I went down at an angle so as to take advantage of the low-growing brambles, gorse, and bracken to check the helter-skelter that might develop. At the bottom of the field is a stile, and beyond it the climb is again helped by the steps that have been cut – though it is obvious that this section could be very tricky when muddy or frozen. The Path traverses a pasture which, surprisingly, is not fenced on the seaward side.

There are a few clumps of bushes here and there, but apart from
that no check before the cliff edge where cows were lying.
Another fence with a stile, and another pasture, with a view of
tree-topped sides to a valley, leading down to another stile and a
yellow Path arrow. Down yet another sloping pasture to a stile
and a Coast Path sign, pointing left, and not, as you might expect,
right down the steps through undergrowth to the beach that lies
at the end of the valley, which is a jungle. At the end of a field is a
stile. DO NOT CROSS IT because there is a very clear yellow arrow
there, and on the stile itself a Coast Path sign. Immediately to the
right there is a narrow wooden footbridge; the water flowing
beneath can be heard but not seen through the undergrowth.
Beyond the bridge a sign shows that the Path goes to the right,
through a very sheltered fertile valley streaked with lines of
cabbages. There is a stiff climb through the pasture to a sign at
the top bearing the acorn, and then a very steep descent to a rusty
barbed-wire fence on the seaward side. I was most glad of this
because a strong wind kept pushing me against it, rather than
over the edge.

At the top of another stiff climb is a National Trust sign, on
Higher Dunscombe Cliff which is sheep pasture. Cross a stile,
there is a field on the left (which had just been ploughed when I
walked there, showing great flints brought to the surface) and on
the right are scattered bushes through which the sea is still just
visible. So are the eastern clifftops, no longer red but orange, and
whited by outcrops of chalk. I was thirsty, and being too lazy to
get out my water bottle, I took elderberries from the hedges along
here: that tangy flavour is certainly a thirst-quencher, and
arouses in me powerful childhood memories. In the next dip
stands a post which, when I was there, had no sign attached to it.
It is clear which way to go, because one way leads straight over the
edge of the cliff, leaving the alternative more likely.

The Path drops to a wooded combe called Weston Mouth,
where another path goes down to a small pebbly beach into which
the Weston stream runs. The western side of this combe is very
strange. An ash tree grows in a deep hollow, hawthorn, giant
brambles, and a little bracken and gorse drop away to the left, and
there are spoil-heaps from former lime-workings – the flints that

were brought to the surface and discarded. After a sharp climb from Weston Mouth and across a field, the Path levels out along the top of Weston Cliff, bearing inland. Keep an eye open along here for a stile, a new one marked with a yellow arrow way down in a hedge overhung with trees, and pointing to the left. Just beyond the hedge is a Coast Path sign which showed me very clearly where I had come from and where I hoped to go; and along the Path down to the right is a carefully cut sign marked 'Coast Path' that some kind well-wisher has put up to keep one going in the right direction. The Path climbs steeply again beneath ash trees and flanked by bracken, and at the top of a short rise is another sign at the edge of a quite wide track, at a point where there are signs of an ancient encampment – perhaps as late as Roman – almost at the edge of the cliff, the present-day cliff anyway.

Follow this wide farm track, a green road pointed out by blue splashes of paint on rocks along the way. The top of the hill is hummocky, and covered with bracken and gorse. Just above the path is a great collection of flints left over from lime-burning – a kind of flint garden. As nothing grows on this, it remains greyish white and can be seen, I imagine, from a long way out to sea. Walking now becomes very easy and pleasant, little rises and falls on a broad green path with, to the left, a broken landscape of green hummocks and hawthorn bushes, with old man's beard frothing over everything.

The green footpath continues, with many mounds and hillocks from the old flint workings, and then follows more closely the line of the cliff edge. The cliffs themselves become much more grey and white. A short sharp drop brings you to a turfy semicircle where there is a bench, much twisted and deformed by rain and sun. An outcrop of rock at this point provides a fine natural viewpoint. I think there must have been some kind of building here formerly, possibly let into the rock and probably an army pillbox, or something similar, perched right on the edge of the cliff for observation purposes. The undercliff is very green, with tall trees in it.

From the signpost at this spot, although the arm had been

broken off, it was clear that the Path goes to the left, along a wooded path with a sharp drop to the combe on the right. This brings you to a path in the combe where there is no indication which way you should go; but you turn right and go downhill towards the sea. About fifty yards down the path is a stile, and beside it another post from which the Coast Path arm has been torn off. Then down through thick woods, at the bottom of which there is some new fencing and a new stile, after which you come out into the open, bearing towards the sea over uneven and rough pasture. Away to the left are lovely slopes, steep, covered with bracken and studded with silver birch. At the foot of this pasture, when I was there, stood yet another splintered and empty signpost, a stile, and steep steps down to the shore.

At the bottom of the path, where the little stream makes its way through a bramble thicket to immolate itself in the shingle, there are two beach huts. Very smartly painted in green, white and black, they have a notice saying: 'This is Private Property. Any Trespassers will be Prosecuted'. Above the name 'The Glen', the Union Jack flies as proudly as above any Victoria Hotel but in this case it flies over what I guessed was a freshwater tank, topped by a television aerial. Here a sign designates the 'Sidmouth Coastal Path' and another little stream burbles out, fringed on both sides by reeds, beside the former fishermen's huts of all shapes and sizes. Outside one of them I saw an elderly couple digging in the garden beyond which is the shingle and a board warning: 'Beware of Adders'.

There are rocks on the shore, and offshore too; and a steep shelving pebble beach. The cliffs are reddish, striped with grey-blue clay, topped by yellow and white chalk, and everywhere are little waterfalls. Going down to the beach and zigzagging up again at Littlecombe Shoot, one passes carefully hidden houses set into the cliff face. This is a gratuitous detour but one which I enjoyed very much. In one of the sheltered gardens of a well-nigh imperceptible house, I saw a cypress, pampas grass, and rioting Iceberg climbing roses.

Once on top of the cliffs again, the Path crosses a wide pasture to a farm gate with a Coast Path sign and an arrow to the right along a cart-track sloping gently downwards, with high banks on either side. The next gate had a most ingenious fastener – the handle of a bucket was fixed to the gatepost to hook over the end of the gate. Beyond this one finds a very pretty open space of turf dotted with hawthorn. And then, suddenly coming into sight, there is an amazing square crenellated tower that looked to me at first like that of a fortified Scottish house. It is Branscombe church, and the view from this down, just behind Berry Cliff, shows the village straggling along its combe – Brendon's or Brannoc's? – making a picture that every town-dweller and foreigner thinks of as typically English – village church, thatched roofs, trees, seclusion. In fact, Branscombe is typical of nothing but Branscombe.

I met on the down a very pleasant woman being walked by her golden Labrador. She told me that the houses I had seen buried in their cliffside seclusion above Littlecombe Shoot were holiday places, and that nobody as far as she knew lived there throughout the year. The water is piped from streams, and there used to be many more chalets further west at Weston Mouth, now National Trust land, all having both electricity and telephone, until a cliff-fall buried the lot.

To the right of this farm track the ground is hummocked and terraced where it was once worked for limestone. To the left there are woods of ash, hazel, and beech, and a sharp drop to the bottom of the combe and Branscombe. Further on, great spreading beech trees grow on the landward sloping combeside. A steep path of sorts goes down through the beechwood to a couple of stiles, over a plank bridge, and across the field directly into Branscombe churchyard. Close to, however, the church looks nothing like a Scottish baronial house. Dedicated to St Winifred – showing its Celtic origins – the Norman crossing-tower is Saxon at the base. There are box pews, a fine eighteenth-century three-decker pulpit; and of the wall-paintings of the Seven Deadly Sins the only one to survive is Lust, as probably it always does. There is a memorial to Joan Tregarthin who died in 1583: she had two husbands, John Keleway and John Wadham, and bore twenty children, fourteen to the first and six to the second.

Church Living – a house opposite the church in Branscombe

They are portrayed kneeling opposite one another. One of the
Wadham sons, Nicholas, founded Wadham College, Oxford in
1610. He did not live to see the college built, but his widow
carried out his wishes and handed over the money which he had
saved for that purpose.

There are two large and ancient yew trees in the churchyard
and a seat on which one may contemplate the beauty of the
tree-covered combeside. Opposite the church is a house called
Church Living, mostly sixteenth-century, but parts of it dating
back as far as the thirteenth century. There are various
explanations of the name – that visiting clerics used to stay there,
or that the name 'Living' means a small farm in Devon and that
the house and land belonged to the Canons of Exeter, i.e., that it
was a Church Farm.

Walking along the road down the hill one passes some attractive colour-washed houses with a wide variety of windows, some wedge-shaped and sticking out like prows rather than bay-windows. Further down, there is a collection of fairly new houses, white-painted and roofed with buff tiles, giving them a Scandinavian appearance. Overlooking these, and set on the side of the hill, are older-style council houses whose porches and doors are painted in a rainbow of gay colours. There is not much point in walking around the bend in the road at this point, and I took the first gate to the right over a meadow to the road beyond. The path across the meadow leads into a farmyard where the confluence of two little streamlets is crossed by stepping-stones. When I got closer to them I found that the houses of 'Scandinavian' appearance are in fact built of brick painted white – and none the worse for that – and that the multi-coloured doors belong to Trafalgar Terrace. Shades of 'England Expects'?

The Coast Path takes the clifftop route through trees to Branscombe Mouth, but if you go into Branscombe village – in addition to the church and Church Living there is an old thatched bakehouse, a forge of great age, and the Mason's Arms, a pub which was originally old cottages – a footpath, starting close to the pub, leads to Branscombe Mouth about half a mile away. The Path goes by way of a Tudor farm with the delightful name of Great Seaside, guarded by a venerable holm oak. A National Trust sign here points to a 'Footpath to cliffs and Beer' and this route follows a cart-track over a cattle-grid. At Branscombe Mouth is a strange-looking thatched building where teas, soft drinks and so forth may be bought during the summer. Further up the farm track is another cattle-grid and a gate.

The Coast Path presents alternatives here. One path goes through a caravan and bungalow settlement – there is a right of way – and the other picks its way none too easily through the rough ground and frequently thick vegetation of the undercliff. My feeling is that the clifftop route is preferable unless there is a particular reason, such as great interest in geology, to make one choose the undercliff route. There is, to my way of thinking, quite enough undercliff walking further east along the Coast Path without embracing it here.

By the top route, there is a stiff climb to the top of Hooken Cliffs and then even going for the next half-mile to the Coast Guard lookout at Beer Head, the most westerly chalk outcrop in the British Isles, rising 300 feet above the sea. If the weather is clear, it is possible to look back to Start Point and forward to Portland – and to wonder how you ever did it, and how you will manage to do it from here on. I once had these views in both directions, in that early morning clear light, before the rain clouds came in from the west.

On the edge of the cliff at one point there is a rock that looks like the tower of a castle and, where the top of the path is reached, the National Trust East Cliff property ends. The other path, coming up steeply from the undercliff, joins the top path just by the Coast Guard lookout. If you are walking westwards, watch out for the sign, as it gives only the undercliff (or Under Hooken) route; with no indication, as there is at the other end, that there are alternative routes. Now joined into one again, the Path follows the contour of Beer Head and then turns at right angles, almost due north, through a kissing-gate to drop down to the village of Beer.

Beer was at one time a great smuggling centre, and the caves in the chalk cliffs used to store contraband, mostly spirits. It has also for long been a centre for lacemaking – 'Honiton' lace. Beer's quarries – or rather mines, since they run in underground galleries – produced the stone with which Exeter cathedral was built c. 1275–1360. One of these underground quarries is being specially reopened to secure matching stone for the restoration of Exeter cathedral.

Spanish blood is said to run in the veins of the inhabitants of Beer since a Spanish ship, possibly one of the Armada, was wrecked there, and the crew found the village depopulated by plague and set about raising the birthrate. Stone and lace and smugglers all existed, so maybe the fertile Spaniards did as well.

A narrow stream runs through the middle of the main street of Beer which at two points is traversed by stone conduits with pagoda tops dating from about 1700. There are food shops, a

Great Seaside Farm, Branscombe, where the holm oak bows to the west wind

café, and a post office here, and Western National bus service
number 497 between Seaton and Sidmouth passes this way.
There is a youth hostel at Beer, and two hotels, the Anchor and
the Dolphin.

Beer is now almost contiguous with Seaton, divided only by
White Cliff. There is a climb of three-quarters of a mile through
the municipal gardens to Seaton. When the tide is out, it is
possible to avoid this walk down the road by going to the beach at
Seaton Hole and walking until you come to the west end of Seaton
Promenade, which you should stay on, if you are walking on
regardless, until you come to the bridge over the Axe at the
eastern end.

Seaton grew up as a seaside resort later than Sidmouth, and it
reflects the Victorian and Edwardian ages in its architecture.

Beer – at one time a centre for lacemaking and smuggling – with a rainbow on the hill

Look out for the Victorian Gothick house on the seafront called 'St Elmo'. In the town itself there is a fine example of imaginative private enterprise. British Rail used to link Seaton Junction on the Axminster-Honiton line to Seaton. The line was closed in 1966 but Modern Electric Tramways Ltd, which had formerly operated in Eastbourne, obtained the right to run trams between Seaton and Colyford on the A35. The tramway opened in 1970 and runs – on the rails brought from Sierra Leone! – along the Axe Estuary, a natural sanctuary for a wide variety of wildfowl which can be observed from the leisurely tramway.

Seaton's church of St Gregory has a thirteenth-century window, but has been altered, 'restored', and generally changed so that little remains of interest. But there are two tombstones worth

The tramway at Seaton: a leisurely journey along the Axe estuary

looking for. One is that of Jack Rattenbury, a famous smuggler
working at the end of the eighteenth century and the beginning of
the nineteenth century along this part of the coast, who published
his *Memoirs of a Smuggler* in 1837. He was born at Beer in 1778
and went to sea as a boy, being taken prisoner by the French and
spending some time in Bordeaux. After his return to seafaring he
was captured again – this time by a Spanish privateer which took
him to Vigo, where he was set free to return to South Devon and
resume his career as a smuggler. The other gravestone also
commemorates a man of Beer, John Starre, whose
sixteenth-century house still stands at the north-west end of Beer
Street. Here is the wonderful punning epitaph that sent John
Starre on his way:

JOHN STARRE
Starr on Hie.
Where should a Starr be
But on Hie?
Tho underneath
He now doth lie
Sleepinge in Dust
Yet shall he rise
More glorious than
The Starres skies.
    1633

17 Seaton to Lyme Regis

When leaving Seaton there is no alternative to crossing the Axe by the 1877 concrete bridge, cunningly fashioned to simulate stone. Stay on the right-hand side of the road and keep a sharp eye for the drive leading to the Axe Cliff Golf Club, which is also the Coast Path and climbs past the club-house and over the edge of the course. Take a gate that leads into a lane with high hedges on both sides, and continue until you reach a sign pointing the way over flint-strewn pastures on the right. Cross fences by two stiles, and then you will come to the entrance to the Landslip which has been a National Nature Reserve since 1955.

At both ends of the Landslip are warning notices, and it should *not* be entered except by experienced walkers. It is nearly 6 miles long, and half a mile wide, and there is only one possible exit from it about half-way along. Much of the route is rough going, especially when it is muddy, and the yellow waymarks must be followed carefully as there is real jungle on both sides: in any case, a nature reserve is there to be cherished and respected.

Dowlands Landslip is exactly what its name suggests. The porous topsoil on the cliffheads became waterlogged and the land just slipped off the limestone below, the largest fall being on Christmas Eve 1839 when some 20 acres of Dowlands Farm fell towards the sea and left a ravine 150 ft deep and 300 ft wide. A reef lifted out of the sea to 50 ft, extending the high-water mark outwards by almost 500 ft.

Since then there has been little or no attempt to clear or cultivate the Landslip. Trees, undergrowth and fauna have flourished untouched by human hand, insecticides or fertilizers. A leaflet on the Landslip is available at the Information Office on Seaton seafront or from the local council offices.

At the entrance to the Nature Reserve, a signpost points to Seaton in the west and Lyme Regis in the east. The Path descends sharply by steps between overhanging brambles and ivy-festooned hawthorns, with yellow paint-marks on the trees and on some posts along the way. There is a tangle of undergrowth in spring and summer, and in the autumn the brambles produce enormous juicy blackberries. There are spindleberry, hawthorn, wayfarer's tree, ash, and long tendrils of ivy, braided thick as ships' hawsers, hanging from branches and twisting around earlier strands until in some cases they are nearly a hundred feet in length – real Tarzan transport. Now and then a great chasm gapes like a disused quarry, the chalk gleaming yellowish-white behind the purple elderberries hanging on trees growing out of cracks in the rock. Crab-apple trees and alder spring from the hollows in which surface water is trapped. The path undulates ceaselessly; great care must be taken when it is muddy, and you should watch for fallen branches, roots and straying brambles.

Where, at one point, the path opens out to bleached and crumbling stone underfoot and one looks up at the rock face and the tangled undergrowth, it is almost like the Corsican *maquis*, yet neither so high nor so thick as the *maquis* where I once got stuck when coming down from a mountain ridge in north-west Corsica. There is a notice: 'National Conservation Corps volunteers are undertaking management work for the benefit of the area and the public. The National Conservation Corps is administered by the British Trust Conservation Volunteers, Zoological Gardens, Regent's Park, London NW1 4RY.' Beyond this point the path moves into a forest of tall ash, with hazel thickets below into which the sun barely penetrates. The ivy still astonishes by its strength and profusion, cascading from the upper branches of the trees. The light is dappled soft green, and underfoot is bracken and a

The Coast Path above Axmouth; looking over Seaton Bay to Beer Head

few nettles, oddly cheering in their familiarity in this virgin forest.

It is difficult to sense just how high above the sea one is when travelling along this path, particularly as it goes up and down all the time. For most of the way through the Landslip one does not hear the sea, whose sound is muffled by the seaward ridge of the edge of the Landslip running between sea and path. Again the path traverses thick ash woods, and once more ivy grows everywhere. When the path opens out, there are great slabs of white cliff on the left, and the ash trees are smaller, with tumbled broken ground filled with brambles, and nettles dominating the undergrowth, until you reach a gladeway to a track below All Hallows' School to which the main entrance is from the A3052 Lyme Regis-Colyford road in the village of Rousdon.

Here the woods change to beech and a footbridge leads over a little stream, on the bank of which are the ruins of a building known as Annie's Cottage and of which practically nothing remains but a slender red-brick chimney. A farm track continues eastwards but the Coast Path, which is clearly marked, climbs steeply up into the woods to undulate again between thick beds of nettles. The landscape reverts to what it was before the slight break at Annie's Cottage – cliffs rearing to the left with undergrowth-filled gullies at their foot and tall trees garlanded with ivy.

Suddenly the path is bordered by a drystone wall on the right and you are among chestnut trees and conifers. The path broadens and there is a notice about the Nature Reserve: 'Axmouth-Lyme Regis undercliffs. Please help to preserve and protect this reserve, its wild life and natural creatures. Coastal Path from Pinhay Cliffs to Ware follows the yellow marks. It is dangerous to leave the path because there are many hidden falls and cliff edges. Access to other parts of the reserve is by permit only: Apply to Nature Conservation Council, Telephone Taunton 0823–83211.'

There are water pipes on both sides of the Path as it opens out and descends to a green-painted corrugated-iron pumping station with busy-sounding machinery inside. The track runs through park-like beech woods, and forks in a slight clearing among the trees. Take the right-hand fork: when I was there, I had some doubt until I went along the track to the first yellow mark on a tree. Further along are more crab-apple trees, and a variety of oaks including some hybrids with elongated pinnate leaves. The Path winds, goes up and down, up a bank over exposed tree-roots, and through damp woods of plane and sycamore where streamlets gush out from under the path and at one point run into a pond lower down on the right. Where we come into the open again there are ash trees dotted around in very tall bracken. Just beyond Underhill Farm, which is to the right of the path, and with Chimney Rock on the left, the Path meets a macadam road and the Nature Reserve and the county of Devon are now behind us. A signposted path across fields brings us out on to the down above the Cobb, Lyme Regis's harbour.

Beyond Lyme Regis, orange cliffs run eastwards to Golden Cap, stretching into the distance along the Chesil Beach to Portland, sitting hull down in the sea and visible from almost every part of the Dorset Coast Path, which starts here at Lyme Regis.

The Dorset Coast Path

1 Lyme Regis

Ralph Wightman, a great man of Dorset, wrote of the main road 'that turns a corner above Lyme Regis to the best sea view in England. The little town is far below – actually only 500 feet below, but this is a big drop for a main road in half a mile. Straight ahead is the most wonderful coastline, stretching for twenty miles to Portland Bill. The great cliffs are broken by half a dozen little combes, and no two cliffs are of the same colour. The highest of them all, 617 feet, is Golden Cap, and in the sunlight its cap is bright gold.'

Lyme Regis takes the first part of its name from the little river Lim, and the second part from its enfranchisement by Edward I in 1279, when it became one of the first loyal and ancient boroughs in the land. But earlier than that, in AD 774, Cynewulf, King of West Saxony, granted land at the mouth of the Lim (or Lym) to the Abbey of Sherborne for the purposes of salt boiling, and the Domesday Book recorded that fourteen saltmen were working there 300 years later. The Cobb (the origin of its name is unknown and is a source of endless speculation) was built during the reign of Edward I: a semi-circular stone breakwater which provided Lyme Regis with a harbour. Henry VIII made a number of grants for the upkeep of the Cobb, and Elizabeth I renewed the town's charter on condition that the Cobb be kept in good repair. In 1347 Lyme fitted out four vessels and sent 62 men to the siege of Calais. But there were return matches when the French raided and burned Lyme Regis several times during the reigns of Henry IV and Henry V. With the threat of the Spanish Armada, Lyme sent two fully manned ships to join the English fleet, and at that time the town's shipping was recorded as being one-sixth that of London.

The town was at its most prosperous in the late sixteenth and early seventeenth centuries when it traded with Spain, Portugal, the East Indies, the West Indies, and also with the West African coast. With the coming of the Civil War, Lyme Regis declared for Parliament and was fortified and defended by women and men alike, making in all a garrison of 600. Prince Maurice's force of nearly 5,000 was unable to force an entrance into the town. One of the defenders, promoted to the rank of colonel, was Robert Blake, later to become famous as an admiral. Parliament granted a sum of £2,000 and a supply of boots and shoes to the town – perhaps to keep the burghers on their Cromwellian toes. When, on the morning of 11 June 1685, the Duke of Monmouth, son of Charles II and Lucy Walters, landed with the intention of leading an insurrection against his uncle James II, he knelt on the shore and 'thanked God for having preserved the friends of liberty and pure religion from the perils of the sea, and implored the divine blessing on what was yet to be done by hand'. The local population flocked to his support, but after the defeat at Sedgemoor twelve Lyme men were hanged on the exact spot where Monmouth had landed. One man who had joined Monmouth and was not caught and brought before Judge Jeffreys, was Daniel Defoe. One cannot be certain of what

Looking down on the Cobb at Lyme Regis, where the South Devon and the Dorset Coast Paths meet

experiences he had, because he always thought it prudent to remain quiet about this episode in later life.

Lyme Regis declined further as a port during the War of the Spanish Succession in the early eighteenth century, and many houses fell into decay. The popularity of sea-bathing revived its fortunes at the end of the eighteenth century, and by 1750 Lyme had become a rival to Bath. Jane Austen enjoyed Lyme Regis and it was there that she wrote and set part of *Persuasion*, in 1815. It is said of Tennyson that when he visited Lyme and was about to have the site of Monmouth's landing pointed out to him, he replied: 'Don't talk to me of Monmouth, but show me the place where Louisa Musgrave fell.' The place can still be seen, for the steps are firmly there, those steps where: '. . . all were contented to pass quietly and carefully down the steep flight, excepting Louisa; she must be jumped down them by Captain Wentworth. In all their walks, he had to jump her from the stiles; the sensation was delightful to her. The hardness of the pavement for her feet, made him less willing upon the present occasion; he did it, however; she was safely down, and instantly, to show her enjoyment, ran up the steps to be jumped down again. He advised her against it, thought the jar too great; but no, he reasoned and talked in vain; she smiled and said, 'I am determined I will:' he put out his hands; she was too precipitate by half a second, she fell on the pavement on the Lower Cobb, and was taken up lifeless!' Well, lifeless for a while, anyway.

Even today Lyme Regis has much of the character of a late-Georgian seaside resort. In Broad Street the Royal Lion and the Three Cups Hotels display their columns and bow windows, and the Esplanade has a Regency bow here and there among the cottages and Victorian villas. In the Philpot Museum in Bridge Street there is a display of arms and cannon-balls from Lyme's military past, and inevitably a fossil collection – for it was twelve-year-old Mary Anning of Lyme who found in 1811 the fossil of the ichthyosaurus, now in the British Museum of Natural History. She went on working in the district until her death in 1847, and among her other chief discoveries were a plesiosaurus and the first pterodactyl skeleton ever to be found in Britain

2 Lyme Regis to West Bay

From the Museum take the bend up Church Street and thence up
the hill of the Charmouth road (A3052). Look out for the
cemetery on the left, about a mile beyond the edge of the town.
Take the lane opposite, and when you come to a gate across the
track take the footpath leading off to the right and up through
woods to the ridge at the top of Timber Hill. The path is steep
and slippery when wet (which it often is, being flanked in summer
by tall bracken, dank undergrowth and elder), and it comes out
beside the Lyme Regis Golf Course. Here too, in summer, the
going is through waist-high bracken, tall foxgloves, and a
profusion of knapweed and gorse. When the path comes out into
the open on the clifftop, you look down on Black Ven, a landslip
area and nature reserve that appears impenetrable (there is no
public access anyway), with bramble and gorse and bushes packed
tightly into the undercliff lying between the present cliff-face and
the sea. It was at Black Ven that Mary Anning chipped the
ichthyosaurus out of that grey rock containing iron pyrites which,
in the eighteenth century and at the beginning of the present
century, caused enough oxidation for the bituminous shale to
smoulder and smoke, and earned the area such fanciful names as
the Lyme Regis Volcano.

At low tide it is possible to walk from Lyme Regis to Charmouth
along the beach, and one can look up at The Spittles, Canary
Ledges and Black Ven, all now in the keeping of the National
Trust. The top route is lined by new bungalows and houses, all
seemingly owned by prize-winning gardeners, and the lane on
which they stand comes out on to a road. This road, Old Lyme
Hill, carries on down to Charmouth and the A35 becomes the
main street of the village. Follow this to just past St Andrew's
Church (1836–38), where you take a turning to the right called
Lower Sea Lane. But take a good look at Charmouth – Regency
and Early Victorian in character but much fussed in summer by
the traffic along the main road. On his Puritan-dodging tour
through the West Country, Charles II is said to have spent a night
in the Queen's Arms Hotel where, a century and a half earlier in
1501, Catherine of Aragon also stayed, her presence being

recorded by marking her badge in the plaster of one of the bedrooms.

Down Lower Sea Lane is an astonishing hut that sells teas – astonishing in that it is painted like a Union Jack and has a somewhat mystifying notice in the window reading 'All Cans are served cold'. (Are 'All Can'ts served hot'?) There is a house called 'Hill View', and a little further along, not to be outdone, another house named 'Hall View' because it faces the village hall, forty or fifty years old, with much creosoted timber hanging about it.

At the bottom of Lower Sea Lane is a narrow footbridge over the River Char which, before it gives up entirely and sinks into the shingle of the shore, broadens into a respectable pool whose contents look more like char than water. Beyond the bridge, the Path climbs steeply to the east and the clifftop above Cain's Folly, where golden-red soil is exposed by cliff-falls. Then, in a hollow, is Westhay, a farm lying under the southern slopes of Stonebarrow Hill which is the north-eastern boundary of the National Trust Golden Cap Estate. The Path crosses two little streams, Westhay Water and Ridge Water, before turning inland around the landslip at Broom Cliff. Just beyond the footbridge across Ridge Water, and some hundred yards inland, are the ruins of Ridge Barn which, if you are watching the map, could be confused with the ruins of St Gabriel's Church. The barn ruins are surrounded by brambles, giant thistles, tall foxgloves and some crouching rose bushes, probably cultivated originally but now gone feral, blooming low down and almost on the ground. Further inland is a house so startlingly white that it reminded me of houses on the Scottish coasts; this is Upcot Farm and for those who want to leave the Path (or to reach it) there is a track leading to Morcombelake village and another to the A35 west of the village.

The Golden Cap Estate, of nearly 2,000 acres, has come to the National Trust since 1961 in the form of land given by individuals or bought through funds provided under the Enterprise Neptune Appeal. On the west of the Estate, 480 feet high on Stonebarrow, the old stone radar-station base-camp was taken over in 1976. One room has been converted into an information centre and shop, and the remainder has been adapted for groups of volunteers who wish to help the National Trust. There are four cottages on the Estate called Ash, Elm, Oak, and Beech and there are some flats at Westhay. Book well in advance, should you think of staying there, either by telephone (Chideock 628) or by writing to Mrs M.J. Easton, Filcombe Farmhouse, Morcombelake, Bridport. The cottages are at St Gabriel's Farmhouse on an acre of land called St Gabriel's Bank, a Dorset Naturalist Trust Nature Reserve dedicated to the preservation of indigenous flora. Just beyond St Gabriel's House is St Gabriel's Church, consecrated in the thirteenth century but now in ruins. It was the parish church until 1841, when a new church was built in Morcombelake village two miles to the north, a village that has developed much during the present century, mostly as a place for retired people. Morcombelake has no lake (its name made up of *mor* – barren, swampy land; *cumb* – valley; and *lacu* – stream; all from Old English). The village lies under Hardown Hill, almost 700 feet high, and the snug and unobtrusive houses are set into the lower slopes of the hill along little lanes that zigzag up from the main road. There is a famous old-established bakery, Moores, in Morcombelake, baking, among other biscuits and cakes, Dorset Knobs – crisp and the size of a golf-ball, so beloved by Thomas Hardy when eaten with a bit of Dorset Blue Vinny cheese. They are light to carry when walking, although a bit bulky – and take care to keep the crumbs out of your sleeping-bag.

The church at Morcombelake is now the village church of Stanton St Gabriel, and it is difficult to find out why the settlement at Stanton died out. There were always stories of smuggling, and rumours that the now-ruined church was used for hiding brandy, so perhaps the Coast Guards and Excisemen made it too tough a place to live in – or maybe a cliff-fall made landings on the coast impossible and so the village just died.

The Coast Path keeps close to the cliff edge up the steep slope to the top of Golden Cap, which is the highest point on the whole south coast of England. You can take your choice from a variety of heights given in books and on maps. I have seen everything from 611ft to 625ft, as well as the roughly approximate and boringly newfangled 191 metres. A good average is 619 ft. The name comes from the golden Upper Greensand or Foxmould that caps the blue and grey lias of Wear Cliff, which has slipped downwards again and again so that the cliff face is a series of blurred steps, made as successive falls of thousands of tons at a time slid off the inner clay. The name of the cap, as Ralph Wightman said, is not fanciful: at all times it is lighter than the cliff below and, according to the weather, is anything from buff to ochre. It is in the early morning sunshine or in the early evening of a clear sunny day that Golden Cap gleams its purest gold.

Golden Cap may be reached from the A35, and in summer many visitors walk the mile or so from the point where cars are left. Consequently the heathy summit is somewhat eroded, but it recovers quickly in winter if there are wet and mild periods. Watch your step down the eastern slope of Golden Cap because this too is eroded and has holes hidden by gorse, heather, and head-high bracken.

During the wars against Bonaparte a lookout station on top of Golden Cap was manned by the Sea Fencibles, and later by Coast Guards, but I have never found any trace of where it used to stand. The view still is much as it must have been at that time – a few more landslips to the west, but the same outlines of Cain's Folly, Black Ven, the white of houses in Lyme Regis, Beer Head in Devon and – if it is very clear – Start Point and the way from which the eastward-walker has come. When all that can be seen, as well as the view to the east along the Chesil Beach to the crouching outline of Portland, which is the next stage of the journey, then the whole walk seems a visible as well as a rewarding achievement.

After an initially steep and rough descent, the Path evens out into a bowl in the downs, where there is bare close-cropped turf, with an occasional hawthorn or pine, bent and scoured by the salt-laden and remorseless sou'westerlies. Cross the stile in the barbed-wire fence where there is a Coast Path sign, and continue about half a mile down to Seatown, the last few yards of the way being helped by steps to the road that ends at the Anchor Inn.

Seatown is no town and certainly not a port. Its name is a

corruption of that ubiquitous Saxon *ton*, meaning a farm, i.e. a farm by the sea. A little stream called the Wynreford, Winneford or sometimes the Chid, makes its way here from the hills in the north, only to form a tired pool and sink into the shingle within sight of the sea. Today there are still a few fishing-boats drawn up into this aborted estuary, but a couple of centuries ago there used to be thirty or forty fishermen here – 'at least', writes John Eastwood in *The Chideock and Seatown Book*, 'they were fishermen by day, but by night they were smugglers, and many a contraband cargo was run in here . . . there were wild rushes to the West Rocks below Golden Cap when a boatload of liquor was being rowed ashore from a French ship . . . The smugglers at one time had a leader known as 'the Colonel' who organised the trade from Seatown to Charmouth, many cargoes being run in to St Gabriel's lonely beach. Later the contraband would be loaded on to pack horses, to be taken through the Marshwood Vale and further inland by devious bridleways and tracks.'

Contraband alcohol played a large part in the history of Seatown, and entered immortally into fiction when Thomas Hardy described in *The Mayor of Casterbridge* the fair at which Henchard sold his wife when he was drunk on furmity. There was indeed a Whit Monday fair at Seatown where furmity was sold by an old woman who would ask her customers if they wanted 'a drop of speerits' mixed into the hot mixture of barley and raisins – to produce a kind of boozy muesli.

Three-quarters of a mile north on the Lyme Regis-Bridport A35 road is the village of Chideock. It was originally somebody's oak, probably Cedda's, and the name has gone through a dozen spellings, but however it is spelt it is always pronounced 'Chiddick'. Vikings raided along this coast, and later the French did the same, so that there was always a threat from the sea. In 1380 John de Chidocke built Chideock Castle which later passed to the Arundell family through the marriage of a Chideock daughter called Catherine. There is no castle stonework to be seen now but it stood in Ruins Field at the end of Ruins Lane – one of those castles blown up by the Cromwellian troops, in this case in 1645 because the Arundells, Roman Catholics, had held out for the King. The castle changed hands several times before it was eventually 'slighted'. In the reigns of Elizabeth and Charles I five Chideock Catholics were martyred, and the facts of their going are recorded on a plaque set into a wooden cross on the site. In 1802 Lord Arundell sold the manor to his cousin Thomas Weld of Lulworth Castle, and it remains in the keeping of this Roman Catholic family to this day.

From Seatown the Coast Path continues from near the grocer's shop, through the car-park, climbs steeply to the top of Ridge Cliff, then over Doghouse Hill (in summer splashed with purple and gold by spear thistles and ragwort), to the top of Thorncombe Beacon (507 feet). This summit is also topped, like Golden Cap, with Upper Greensand, but there is less of it and the cliff seems less brightly crowned than Golden Cap when seen from a distance. There used to be a military pillbox here, part of Britain's optimistic plans to throw German invaders back into the English Channel. For years the building was a repository for beer-cans, crisp-packets, graffiti, and all the other objects that derelict places attract. It has now been demolished and the clifftop's dignity restored.

I saw a fascinating aerial display there – beyond the edge of the cliff some seagulls were planing and mewing, and between and around them half a dozen jackdaws were flying out to sea, coming back, alighting on the projecting undercliff and taking off again, but keeping always just below the level of the clifftop. And above gulls and jackdaws, a pair of kestrels divided their flight, at times hovering almost motionless, between the very edge of the cliff and a line some hundreds of yards inland. These three species of birds were apparently overlapping one anothers' territory, each going about its business in its own manner, while yet respecting the choreography.

The Path descends towards Eype (pronounced 'Eep') Mouth through fields, some of them cultivated to the very edge of the cliff. In summer, rolled bales of straw stand on the patterned stubble like wool waiting to be knitted. Beyond, the golden serrated cliffs drop into jungly scrub and thickets, bracken and bog, and at the very bottom grey clay oozes its way into the sea:

that same clay off which the topsoil slides, making the landslips of these parts. Looking east, this grey is predominant; until just beyond West Bay there is the golden gleam of Burton cliffs. In the middle distance, looking north-east, is Colmer's Hill, like something out of a Chinese painting – a sudden small conical hill with a tuft of pine trees on the top. It is just to the west of Bridport and can be seen from the town's main street, drawing the eye upwards from the bridge at the bottom of the hill and the houses of West Allington on the other side of it.

At Eype's Mouth a tiny stream comes down through a gap in the cliffs, bubbling over rocks, often coloured when in spate by the blue lias. It loses itself abruptly – as do most of the streams along this stretch of coast – in the shingle of the beach at a point where a few boats are drawn up, and rusty twisted remains of winches, lobster pots and nets in various conditions show that here was, and to some extent still is, a fishing-place. A narrow lane comes down from the main – yet very minor – road to Bridport by way of Eype Village, which is half a mile from the sea: a small stone hamlet with a pub and cul-de-sac of houses called Lower Eype. Close to the sea there is a parking place on top of the cliffs, and also the Eype's Mouth Hotel.

The beach, shingle and sometimes sand, according to the tides, is one of the best in Dorset from which to swim, and at the western end there are boulders so cut and worn by the sea that they stand up from the sand like fragments of some long-buried cathedral. A tongue of rock runs out into the sea to separate Great Ebb from East Ebb Cove, which lies below Thorncombe Beacon. Not that there is much great ebb in evidence here – just a constant trickle of fresh water from pockets of undercliff. Because the cliffs are so difficult to get up to, or down from (I once watched my son and nephew get stuck up there for an hour), there is a wealth of wild life. I have seen a fox there, and what I at first took be be a wildcat but which was more likely a feral tom that had taken to wearing its ears in the low-profile position. There are adders and frogs in the pools which here are free from all spraying or contamination, bog asphodel, common sundew and bog pimpernel grow freely, and kestrels and

Colmer's Hill, just west of Bridport

buzzards hover and circle, often on a level with the clifftop walker.

From Eype's Mouth the Path climbs West Cliff (it is east of Eype, but is Bridport's West Cliff) staying close to the edge of the cliff and to seaward of camping sites. From the top of West Cliff the Path runs gently down towards West Bay and soon passes in front of a line of bungalows. Keep to seaward of them, and of the low green tower.

3 West Bay and Bridport

West Bay was originally called Bridport Harbour and that is what many Dorset people still call it. In fact, the whole of Lyme Bay is the West Bay, and the Harbour was made not by God or nature but by man's repeated and courageous – and some might say

misguided – efforts. Look down from West Cliff and you will see
that there is no natural indentation or haven along this end of the
Chesil Beach, where millions of tons of shingle move endlessly. So
why and how was the Harbour built?

The valley of the Brit (the river from which Bridport takes its
name) and the land around it is excellent for growing hemp and
flax. Since before the Norman Conquest ropes, fishing nets and
cordage of all kinds have been manufactured there. Bridport was
the principal provider of cordage to the Royal Navy from the
time of King John to Queen Elizabeth I's reign, and gave the
nickname of 'Bridport dagger' to the hangman's rope. When
overland travel was difficult owing to rough and muddy roads –
and rough and ready plunderers – the rope had to go by sea to
the Naval shipyards, so a harbour was essential. Originally the
harbour and boat-building yards (where small trading and fishing
vessels were constructed) were further up the Brit, and a channel
was kept free to the sea. This meant constant clearing of silt and
river sand from the stream and pebbles from the outlet. There
has always been the greatest difficulty in getting into the harbour
(now closer to the coast and westward of the original harbour
entrance) between the piers, then built of wood, now of steel and
concrete. Through the years Bridport and its harbour have
fought an unceasing battle against the sea. I can remember many
times when the sea has smashed the piers and the esplanade. In
1974, it flooded the valley of the Brit almost to Bridport town.

The decline of sail before steam reduced the amount of rope
needed by the world, and chiefly by the Royal Navy and the
Newfoundland fishing fleets; and the harbour's trade was further
adversely affected when the Great Western Railway reached
Bridport town in 1857, and Bridport Harbour in 1884, when the
GWR invented the name of West Bay. Now the railway has
vanished from both town and harbour, but the name West Bay
has stuck. Shingle and sand is still shipped out, and wood from
the Baltic is imported. There is a lively fishing business in which
many local men engage while doing other jobs as well – like Peter
Northover, who is the Harbour Pilot, and John Eastwood, writer.

The Coast Path leads around the Harbour by the road across

the bridge over the Brit. On the other side is the Bridport Arms, and a terrace of five houses that looks as if it has been towed over from Dieppe or some other French port. It was designed by E.S. Prior, built about 1885, and now incorporates the Bay House Hotel. The French appearance of the place led to its being used as a training-ground for the Dieppe Raid in 1942.

West Bay is very small and you can walk around it in about fifteen minutes. There is a grocer's store, two other pubs in addition to the Bridport Arms, a butcher, a fishing-tackle store, and assorted shops in the complex lying landward of the short promenade. If the West Bay Hotel looks French, the 1936 church of St John the Evangelist has a white simplicity that is nearly Scandinavian. A stained-glass window of 1959 by Randoll Blacking incorporates the brig *Mary Hounsell*, one of two ships of that name built at Bridport in the early nineteenth century.

Bridport is about 1½ miles to the north, and there are Western National buses 405, 406, 412 to Bridport and Weymouth. Bridport itself is a pleasant town with a museum housed in The Castle (a small building with a sixteenth-century front), a late eighteenth-century rope and net factory, and many interesting seventeenth- to nineteenth-century houses, including Beach the Chemist's which was once the George Inn where Charles II was almost caught on 24 September 1651 during his scamper through Dorset. A stone commemorating his flight is set into the bank at the corner of Lee Lane and the road to Dorchester. The youth hostel is in Allington, across the bridge at the western edge of Bridport on the road to Lyme Regis.

From West Bay quayside the Coast Path continues for a hundred yards along the road running parallel to the sea. Turn right off the road after Sam Gibb the butcher's, and make across the beach towards the foot of East Cliff. On the right is the East Beach Fish Store, where fish is both packed and sold to those who care to go over and ask my old friend Des Gape for a boiled crab or fresh mackerel. Behind the fish store is a vast building, a dark Satanic mill often clamorous with machines and flickering flames, where shingle from the beach is processed, for use in the building trade.

4 **West Bay to Abbotsbury**

The Coast Path climbs to the top of East Cliff which runs to the
seaward side of the Bridport and West Dorset Golf Course which,
like so many golf-courses along the Path, preserves the greenness
of a section of the route near a town. It then drops steeply into a
cleft, rises, then drops again to Freshwater where there is the
large Freshwater Caravan Park with its orderly streets of
caravans, many of them with little cultivated plots for flowers and
vegetables. Here the walker is faced with a choice. You can either
take the footpath inland around the boundary of the caravan
park and cross the little stream, the Bride, by a footbridge; or, as I
have always preferred to do, you can keep to seaward of the
caravans and cross the Bride at one of the places on the beach
where there are stepping-stones. For many years the Bride was a
mere trickle of water sinking into the shingle and a rather
stagnant pool, but recently there has been much bulldozing of the
shingle – to lessen the danger of flooding – into a gravelly canyon,
along the bottom of which the Bride, liberated for the first time in
ages, bubbles merrily to make direct contact with the sea. This
means there is more water to be crossed by stepping-stones or by
wading.

A stile with a yellow arrow painted on it gives a choice of routes:
one path leads through meadows along the southern bank of the
Bride, with the landward side of Burton Cliffs rising between the
path and the clifftop. It is a pleasant enough walk, though
somewhat dull, with the prospect of Burton Bradstock in its
sheltered dell along the valley and at the end of the path a
gateway into a cul-de-sac of thatched houses, one of which is the
Dove, a favourite pub about which I have written in some detail in
Dorset Villages. But there is no reason why this meadow path
should be followed, except when the Bride is in spate or when
there have been sudden and heavy cliff-falls. The other path at
the stile leads sharply to the clifftop and, although thousands of
tons of cliff fall to the beach quite frequently, the path at the time
of writing is both wide and safe. Fenced strongly on the landward
side but not on the seaward side (so keep well clear of the
treacherous edge), the path has a wonderful view out to sea and

along to Portland. This is National Trust territory and three seats, spaced at intervals, face the sea; wonderful when there is an excuse to be found – and there usually is – to relace a boot, tighten rucksack straps, or take a long and careful look at the map. To hell with excuses! Just sit down, take a breather, look out to sea, and give thanks to the National Trust.

There is a third possibility: take an interesting walk along the shore, from where the structure of the cliff can be seen in all its striated browns and golds. In the spring the gull colonies, harassed by bandit jackdaws planning a sudden break-and-entry to eggs and chicks, make loud and unceasing cry. When these cliffs fall massively to the shore below, a field of fossils is often revealed. I have found plenty in the past, mostly ammonites which still decorate my house. In the early sixties my friend the Canadian writer Farley Mowat, who is biologist, ecologist, geologist and practically everything else that involves the study of all that grows in the land and sea about us, stayed for several months in a cottage on the farm where I lived. He found, after a particularly heavy cliff-fall, belonites and some splendid ammonites. Nearly twenty years later he went directly to an ammonite in my house and identified the precise spot under Burton Cliffs where it had been found.

While walking the clifftop Coast Path on this section, I once saw, at half-past six in the morning, what I took to be a heifer, escaped from the other side of the wire to stray perilously close to the cliff edge where it had lain down to sleep. Approaching this supine mass carefully, for fear of scaring it over the edge, I found it was an Army-surplus sleeping-bag wrapped around a sleeping girl, her face, tanned like a Cox's Orange Pippin, framed by dark hair and decorated by long eyelashes. I almost woke her up to give her a cup of Thermos coffee, but she was smiling peacefully through some dream and a morning nightmare would have been too cruel. From beyond the tower of Burton Bradstock church a lemon sun was clambering into the mauve sky that matched the mallow flowers around her: a very sensible and comfortable girl there, about to awaken to a slice – however thin – of worthwhile living.

A macadamed road runs to the shore at Burton Bradstock – or, at least, to the well-planned and well-operated National Trust car-park there. There are lavatories, and a summer tea and ice-cream hut. This road comes from the main Burton Bradstock-Abbotsbury road, and is lined with bungalows and well tended gardens: a road, perhaps, of the retired and itself a retiring road.

Burton Bradstock is a bare half-mile inland from the clifftop route. After the bungalows and the police-station on the left-hand corner, turn left and walk along the main road until you reach Cheney's Garage (which has the only motor showroom I know of set in an orange quarry), turn sharp right over the bridge and you are in Burton Bradstock. Well, almost. There is a post office, a grocery store, three pubs, but yet little of the village on display. The true village exists in the small back roads of stone houses, often thatched, with a village green where a former chapel now serves as the County Library and where the White House bears a tablet dated 1635. Everywhere there are cul-de-sacs, and a wonderful row of cottages where the old mill used to be. Grove Street, Donkey Street, Shadrack Road: Burton Bradstock deserves a leisurely exploration, sympathetic to its manner of growing up. It is still a true Dorset coastal village, and the tourist industry for which it now caters without transplanting its own heart, has in no way disfigured it. There are many new houses, very well designed architecturally but away from the old centre of the village.

From the gap in the cliffs, the car-park and the road leading to it, the Coast Path leads gently up the next cliff, past a somewhat Army-Navy and yet original kind of house, with concrete outriders against the tides. As far as I know or can remember, this house has always been on the winning side and stays there, defying the waves.

The path continues along the low clifftop of Fuller's Earth until it skirts a caravan park which, unlike that at Freshwater, is on high ground and totally unassailable by the sea. This is the old Coast Guard Station park, much smaller than Freshwater but again with caravans in orderly rows, many of them with small

gardens beside them. Once, when bicycling along the shore from
Swyre to Bridport for some crazy but exhilarating reason which I
have now forgotten, I wheeled my bike like a refugee through
these orderly lines, hoping not to be noticed at that very early
hour. One of the occupants was up and about, a teak-faced and
white-moustached man with brilliant blue eyes, ministering to his
snapdragons with a battered green watering-can. It seemed to me
that I was wheeling my way perilously close to his snapdragons
and stocks so I ground out what was meant to sound like just a
passing 'Good morning'. He raised the rose of his watering-can
from his estate and, as it dribbled to a halt, he replied with infinite
courtesy, 'Good mornin', it'll last, I think, don't you?' No
interrogation about my ancient bicycle, or how I came to be there
at that hour, nor about where I was going on a palpably non-Tour
d'Europe route. 'Looks like it!' I replied brightly, teeth and
Sturmey Archer gears rushing into action.

After this caravan park, the cliffs peter out and the flat
coastline and golden ridge of the Chesil Beach really begin. The
vegetation changes too, with tall thistles giving way to sea-beet,
the leaves of which I have gathered along here for years since it is
much better than garden spinach. There are yellow sea-poppies,
large sea-kale and dense carpets of thrift as you come to Cogden
Beach, where what used to be a military road is now reduced to
lines of great potholes between bits of concrete that look nearly as
ancient and interesting as ammonites. Running down parallel to it
is another track, leading to a grassy and often muddy car-park
just before the shingle begins. Sometimes somebody collects the
parking fee, and sometimes ice-creams and drinks are sold from a
van there, but its great advantage is that motorists can reach a
part of the shore which is still relatively deserted except in high
summer (though in nearly all seasons perpetually optimistic
mackerel fishermen sit there the night through with nothing but
their lines running out to sea and their Thermos flasks beside
them). In general, the kind of people who like Cogden's deserted
shore are those who dislike crowds, and as a result the beach is
remarkably free of rubbish and is respected by those who go
there.

Beyond Cogden, a rough but pretty clear track runs between marshy pastures on the landward side and the piled-up shingle ramparts of the Chesil between the walker and the sea, to the right. On the left, weed-beds begin to form and eventually declare their true watery interest: this is Burton Mere, a wild-bird sanctuary usually alive with the cluckings, scoldings, complaints and tick-tockings of the birds that nest and breed there.

For some reason that I cannot understand, the official Coast Path makes a detour to the north, i.e. inland, of Burton Mere. It is no more attractive than the path on the seaward side, and I believe there can be no more danger of disturbing the birds by going on one side rather than the other. But if you stick to the rules and follow the inland path you will see, on the high ground up towards the main road, a clump of conifers surrounding a house now run as a community called Othona. A little eastward there is another well-hidden house. Otherwise there is nothing along this stretch of the Bridport-Abbotsbury ridge road and if, when walking down below, you could not hear the occasional swish of cars and labouring of heavy lorries on the gradients, you might believe that you were many miles from the nearest human activities.

Beyond Burton Mere, at a point where there is a gate, the ditch can be crossed to the seaward side, to reach the path that is parted from the sea by the Chesil pebble ridge. Brambles, clover, ragwort, and thrift are dotted all over the patches of scrubby grass, and on the shingle itself are the bluish-green crinkled leaves of the sea-cabbage. Burton Mere gives way to a somewhat rushy pasture, and if you wish to escape from the harsh monotony of slogging on shingle you can cross by one of the fairly frequent plank bridges to the fields. Dorset horned sheep often graze here, a breed that takes the ram in summer and consequently lambs in December, giving Christmas lamb – another martyr to set beside the turkey.

Once when I was walking along this section of the path in early summer, I crossed a field of newly mown hay just beyond a tarred and corrugated-iron-roofed shepherd's hut; I must have passed close to a lapwing's nest, or to its mate and young, because it started circling, its long, slow, flapping flight alternating with bursts of zigzagging low over my head, crying all the time. It followed me in this way for a good half-mile until it saw me safely away on the rough track that begins alongside some tarred shacks, around which lie bits of fishing and sailing gear. The going becomes easier here, along a rutted grassy track with reeds still on the inland side and the Chesil pebbles still stacked between the walker and the sea. For those who are not continuing along the Coast Path, there is a footpath leading up to Swyre, where there is the Bull Inn and buses to Bridport and Weymouth. By crossing over this main road and taking that going north from the left of the Bull and past the church, you can head by way of Puncknowle (rhymes with 'tunnel') for the youth hostel at Litton Cheney, on the edge of the narrow, bright, little Bride stream and next door to the White Horse pub (3 miles).

West Bexington is scarcely a village, just a few new bungalows and houses, the Old Manor Hotel, the farm next door, and the post office and general store. An even more direct route to the Litton Cheney Youth Hostel goes by way of the track just beyond the Manor House Farm (that is, continue in a straight line instead of following the road round the bend by the post office). This track is, incidentally, the one that one takes if making for the Coast Path Alternative Inland Route (see p.198). The track climbs towards the clearly visible Puncknowle Knoll Coast Guard building, now vandalized and roofless, and carries on to Puncknowle, and a short-cut by way of Look Farm, to the youth hostel. A left turn at the T-junction beyond Look Farm takes you straight there.

But if you are carrying on towards Abbotsbury there is, just before West Bexington and standing on a mound seemingly in the most prominent and vulnerable position that could be imagined, an old World War II pillbox. Then there is the car-park on the seaward side, the café with a cracked and derelict swimming pool on the left, and the road inland that passes the Manor House Hotel, the farm, the post office, and leads uphill to reach Swyre in one mile, going up at an angle and making it much longer than the track route.

For a few hundred yards along the shore beyond the beach car-park at West Bexington, there are huts on the inland side of the park, often with very healthy elderly people pottering around them. The Path continues as a grassy track, grandly named on the OS map as Burton Road, still with the shingle ramparts on the right hiding the sea beyond. Along here are great patches of thrift, yellow sea-poppies, sea-kale, sea-spinach, mallow, and pink or white yarrow.

This is fairly monotonous walking, with sea out of sight and the same level landscape rising sharply further inland to the left. After less than a mile there is a more solid track with Coast Guard cottages on the left; a little further on is Lawrence's Cottage – very self-contained looking, thatched, and nothing to do with either T.E. or D.H.

The path becomes a macadamed road below Castle Farm, which is in the parish of Abbotsbury.

5 Abbotsbury

Abbotsbury Castle, a bivallate Iron Age hill-fort, stands on the ridge of the downs far above the shore and just north of the Bridport-Abbotsbury road. The 'Castle' of Castle Farm was an eighteenth-century house, burned down in 1913. The road just beyond it leads up left through an ilex avenue, on the right of which are the Abbotsbury Sub-Tropical Gardens, with giant magnolias, camellias, and a wide variety of exotic plants sheltered by trees from south-west gales and frost. On what looks like an exposed position at the top of this road where it joins the highway, there is a pretty cottage with a garden that had a palm tree in it which, I fear, *has* suffered some damage by frost.

The public lavatories at the corner of the beach road, and the lifebelts hanging in full view from posts in the shingle, are reminders that the beach here is much visited in summer and that where the thirty-foot pebble ridge shelves steeply to the sea a dangerous undertow lies in wait.

Take a choice of paths into Abbotsbury, one of the most attractive villages in Dorset, its houses of honey-coloured stone often thatched with reeds gathered locally. The road past the

Looking east, through Abbotsbury

Sub-Tropical Gardens (open mid-April to mid-September 1000–1630, Sundays 1400–1800) leads up to the main road. Turn right, and walk the length of Abbotsbury's one and only main street; or pass the end of the road and walk along the shingle path that often serves as a rough car-park for holiday-makers and mackerel fishermen. This track ends in a couple of hundred yards at a patch of scrub, to the left of which is a stile and a Coast Path signpost to a rough farm track bending away inland from the reed-beds (where the thatch comes from). The first signpost points to west and east across the track and is rather quaintly marked 'Permissive Path' – rather like a Primrose Path. It runs from the Sub-Tropical Gardens road, and is a permitted route that the Coast Path walker could take. Ignore it for the moment and continue along the track that has a tamarisk hedge on the left

and a narrow stream on the right, and which soon reaches a Coast
Path sign where those not going into the village turn right.
Ahead, the track forks, and both paths lead into Abbotsbury; the
left-hand one joins the main road close to where the road from
the Gardens comes out, and the right-hand one comes into a lane
which is the route from the village to St Catherine's Chapel.

In Abbotsbury there is the Ilchester Arms, a post
office-cum-general shop, and some smaller shops selling food
and home-grown fruit and vegetables in season. Just east of the
Ilchester Arms is a road signposted 'New Barn and Swannery'.
Down here lies the heart of Abbotsbury. The church, dedicated to
St Nicholas, is on the left of the road. Rebuilt in the early
sixteenth century it has much of interest – an early
thirteenth-century effigy of an Abbot, some good stained-glass, a
plastered tunnel vault, and a fine Jacobean carved pulpit in the

The Great Tithe Barn, Abbotsbury – it dates from about 1400

back of which are two holes, said to have been made by Parliamentary musket balls in 1644. The Abbey, of which some ruins still remain, was founded in 1044 by Orc, one of Cnut's stewards, and his wife Thola. The Benedictines flourished here – and flourished is the word, for the Tithe Barn is 272 ft long, surviving from about AD 1400, and housed the grain from a large area under monastic rule until the Dissolution of the Monasteries in 1539. The lands then passed to Sir Giles Strangways, who built himself a house with the Abbey stones: this house was destroyed in the Civil War when a powder magazine exploded.

St Catherine's Chapel, standing some 250 ft above Abbotsbury, was built entirely of stone in the late fourteenth century, and served as a mark for sailors. There is a signpost to it from the main street, and an address from which the key may be obtained. Not only is the chapel an architectural marvel, but there is a fine sweep of coast to be seen from the top of Chapel Hill – the Chesil Beach, the brackish lagoon called the Fleet that is enclosed by the Chesil, and, immediately below the hill, the Swannery which has been there since at least 1393. More than 500 swans feed on the eel-grass that grows in the Fleet, and they have been cared for during the last 200 years by members of the Lexster family, until John Fair took over from Fred Lexter in 1980.

6 Abbotsbury to Weymouth

Whether coming east from the Coast Path or south down the farm-track from Abbotsbury village, the signpost in the hedge points the way clearly over a stile into a rising pasture on the lower southern slopes of Chapel Hill. This is preferable to the Permissive Path, because it is higher (and therefore drier) and has a better view of the Swannery and the Fleet.

Over the crest of the flank of the hill, just past an old Second World War concrete pillbox, some houses and trees come into sight, and at a hedge there is a farm stile over to the track leading from the Swannery car-park to the Swannery itself (open daily mid-May to mid-September). Turn left up to the car-park, where there are lavatories when the Swannery is open, then right on to the metalled road for a hundred yards to where there are some

farm buildings. A Coast Path sign points the way through a farm
gate by a Dutch barn, immediately beyond which is a waymarked
stile on the right. Climb up to the ridge of Linton Hill, where
there is a double stile between two barbed-wire fences that replace
a collapsed drystone wall. Looking around from here, down on
the right you see the dark mass of Nunnery Grove, straight back
to the west is St Catherine's Chapel, and down on the coast below
the Swannery, a palette of water divided from the sea by the Chesil.

The Path continues along the ridge and ahead, a little off to the
right, is Portland, from here apparently a true island and well out
to sea. The Path drops sharply seawards through a hillside
covered with gorse and bramble. At the bottom of the hill two
mahogany-coloured donkeys with white-patched faces followed
my progress with keen attention, until I passed out of their sight
and stood above Clayhanger Farm where red, blue and striped
sheets danced on the washing line in the stiff west wind like
Ballets Russes dancers in Bakst costumes. Above Clayhanger a
Coast Path signpost marks Abbotsbury 1 mile, ahead to East Fleet
4 miles, and to the left a public footpath to the Abbotsbury-
Portesham road.

Cross the stile in the fence on the left and the path continues
over downland pasture, across a farm track running from the top
of the down to Clayhanger Farm, over another stile, and then
carries on along the ridge. Just before some hillside scrub there is
a stile into pasture on the left, and by walking a little higher on the
flank of the down the Hardy Monument (see p.201) comes on to
the skyline. At the next stile through a hedge there is a partly
fallen drystone wall, with a well preserved piece on the left
showing the art of fine wall-construction with flat stones. On the
far side of the next stile is a narrow pasture – its narrowness
seemed just as well, since there was a Hereford bull there with 20
Friesian heifers. He chewed his hay placidly, and I was tempted to
pat him on his ringless nose, but resisted.

On the far side of the next pasture there is a sign along a farm
track to the left, to West Elworth; over the stile and to the right,
East Fleet is $3\frac{1}{2}$ miles. The Path drops between elder and brambles
here, on the lower slopes of Merry Hill, and at the foot of the hill

is a stile, and a path along the left of a hedge that becomes a wood. There is another stile at the far corner of this field, at a point where the Path seems to coincide in wet weather with a lively stream. Beyond that stile turn left, where the Coast Path sign is marked East Fleet 3 miles. Across the valley are the buildings of New Barn Farm and its cottages: formerly, the Coast Path ran along the metalled road from Abbotsbury for two miles and passed through New Barn farmyard.

Another narrow stream is crossed by a stout plank bridge, and less than a hundred yards ahead is the road from the Swannery, nearly invisible unless a vehicle is moving along it. Cross the road and take the stile into the field on the other side, where there is a Coast Path signpost that gives no distances. Climb this gentle hill, on the right of which is Wyke Wood, its treetops bent by the prevailing west wind. At the top turn right along the top edge of Wyke Wood and head towards the now visible Fleet, the Chesil, and the sea. A gradual descent towards solitary Bridge Lane farmhouse, its single chimney pointing to the sky like a finger, brings you to Bridge Lane, which leads to the farmhouse from the Swannery road and runs through Wyke Wood. The Coast Path goes the other way, and keeps left of the hedge in front of the house, leading to a stile and a signpost. Carry on through the next field to a footbridge, beyond which the Path comes to the shore of the Fleet.

In summer here the air is loud with the sound of bumble bees and the popping of gorse pods in the heat which, when there is little wind, is trapped here and makes this isolated place like a pocket in some exotic wilderness. Walk along the bank of the West Fleet to the somewhat battered landing-stage at the end of the road coming from Langton Herring, a village less than a mile up that road. The Elm Tree pub has a restaurant, and there is a post office in the village. In summer, Western National runs an open-top 412 bus along the coast, by way of Rodden and Langton Herring, between Weymouth and Bridport: it may be caught at the Elm Tree. There is a footpath back to the bank of the Fleet from just south of the pub.

Continue along the bank of the Fleet, making sure that the path is followed across the neck of Herbury, a small low-lying promontory that sticks out into the waters of the Fleet. In 1981–2, Herbury was named as a possible site for the next nuclear power station in the West Country.

Keep to the seaward side of a hedge and a barbed-wire fence, and ignore the stile. The route skirts Gore Cove and brings you into the grounds of an hotel now called Moonfleet Manor, formerly known, and still appearing on most maps, as Fleet House. It was originally a house belonging to the Mohun family, Normans who came over with Duke William and whose name has also been corrupted into the name of the village Hammoon on the Stour. The present Fleet House – or Moonfleet Manor – is mostly Georgian and nineteenth-century; it incorporates a pub called the Mohun Arms and the Why Not? Bar (taking its name from the Mohun armorial bearings, which resemble a capital letter Y).

The hotel's present name is a case of life imitating art – in this case, J. Meade Falkner's novel *Moonfleet*, a tale of smuggling in these parts that was first published in 1898. It has gone into many subsequent printings, and has been read as a serial on the wireless and performed on television.

Keep to the shoreline below the hotel, cross the little stream by the footbridge, and keep to seaward of the fence. Inland are cultivated fields in a wide and undulating landscape. The path is clearly marked along this section, and there are two World War II pillboxes with a quarter of a mile between them, their concrete roofs useful for sitting on when the track is muddy, and very good for lying on in the sunshine. They have been nearly absorbed into the landscape, closely embraced by mallow, yarrow, brambles, and ling.

Just over a mile from Moonfleet, the shoreline curves northwards at Butterstreet Cove; a few hundred yards inland is the hamlet of East Fleet, where only the chancel remains of old Holy Trinity Church, destroyed together with most of the village in the storm of 23 September 1824 when the sea breached the Chesil. This storm was called the 'Outrage', and there has been fairly constant fear of a repetition. In 1839, giant waves lifted the

500-ton vessel *Ebenezer* on to the top of the Chesil, and she had to
be refloated in the Fleet and towed to Portland Roads to reach the
sea again. There are two early seventeenth-century brass plates to
members of the Mohun family in the new church of Holy Trinity,
which was built in 1827–9 in a style that still echoed the
eighteenth-century Gothic revival. It has a quiet and secluded air,
and its stone is splotched with red lichen that seems to thrive in
the shade of the surrounding beech trees.

The Coast Path hugs the Fleet shore around Chickerell Hive
Point, where there is a landing-stage and a stile, which is crossed
to follow the Path along the shore of the East Fleet to another
small promontory called Tidmoor Point, somewhat illogically, as
it is more like a potato. Tidmoor is a rifle-range, and when the
red flags are flying there is a notice pointing out that it is
dangerous and that sentries at each end will tell walkers what to
do, and will either signal for firing to stop while the range is
crossed, or will act as escort as well. When the flags are not flying,
you can walk around the low clifftop of the blobby promontory;
but for those who decide to skip the walk through the Weymouth
conurbation, there is a track up to road B3157 at Charlestown,
and a bus service into the centre of Weymouth, two miles to the
east.

7 Weymouth

If you plan to walk to Weymouth, carry on around the edge of
Lynch Cove – there is a busy caravan park there in summer.
Beyond a footbridge, the path goes inland a little towards one of
the narrowest points of the Fleet, to a stile and a diversion around
the Royal Engineers Training Camp Headquarters and Bridging
Hard. Turn right at the end of the barbed-wire fence and walk
down the tarmac road to where a prominent Coast Path sign gives
5½ miles west to Abbotsbury and an unspecified distance east to
Ferry Bridge. Turn left here; the Path climbs gradually to the top
of low cliffs, below which there is tumbled undercliff in which
rabbits have made a warren and hop unconcernedly around
throughout the day. This is a very pleasant walk, nothing like as
urban as one might think from the map or from the rather

cautious descriptions given of it on occasion, including those in some Coast Path guides. The path runs to seaward of pastures which, when I last walked there, were so bright with buttercups, daisies and clover that I almost wished I were herbivorous. A very solid stone boundary-mark states 'Borough of Weymouth and Melcombe Regis 1933' and underneath 'Hambling, Mayor' so there can be no doubt about who was responsible for putting up the stone. Just beyond here the ground to the left changes from that wonderful lush pasture to oozy reed-beds where there is obviously some kind of hidden – at least in the summer – stream making its way down to the Fleet. It is also clear that the Fleet waters can rise considerably, because I saw a farm gate festooned to half its height with dried seaweed.

Follow the line of the low cliff edge to the next stile, which is set beside another old wartime pillbox. The stile is in a hollow which is often very muddy. At this point the cliffs have almost vanished and often there are boys down on the foreshore digging for bait. At the top of the next rise is a notice, white on red, 'Warning to Parents and Children, Keep Out, Danger' above a great metal pipe disgorging something that looks like pure water but probably is nothing of the sort. From here on the outline of Portland dominates the eastward-traveller's view.

Beyond the next fence is the big Blue Waters Holiday Village in which, mercifully, most of the caravans are either green or sand-coloured and blend more or less into the background among the saplings that have been planted in and around the site. Keep to the path seaward of the camp, whose main office and a gallant row of flagpoles gleam above like an outpost of Empire; you will come out on to the Weymouth-Portland A354 road beside the Ferry Bridge pub, whose local name was recognized thus by Devenish the brewers in 1979, after having for a very long time been the Royal Victoria (by which name it appears in most Coast Path guides). Here the Fleet joins the sea at Small Mouth estuary, crossed by Ferry Bridge. On the other side of the road, opposite the pub, there is a clearly marked footpath alongside a factory fence. Less than a hundred yards further on, it comes out on the former railway line that used to link Weymouth and

Portland. You are on the Weymouth side of the Ferry Bridge channel, where a new bridge is due to be constructed across Small Mouth, opening in 1982–3.

In 1944, while preparing for D-Day, the US Army feared destruction of the road bridge by German bombers, and laid a concrete track from Weymouth between, and on either side of, the lines over the railway bridge, to enable tanks and motor transport to reach Portland and the invasion fleet. Now the railway bridge has gone but the concrete track remains along the no longer 'permanent' way. In muddy weather, this is useful to walk along, but much of it runs through a cutting and the sea is out of sight. It is usually better to take the top of the seaward embankment, from which there is a fine view of the harbour and of Portland across the water. This path in summer is bright with buttercups, stitchwort, campion, heath, and spur valerian in shades ranging from dusky pink to deep crimson. There are patches of cow parsley, ragwort, tall melilot, hawthorn, and elder.

Where the path along the embankment ends, and the old railway track is barred to adventurous motorists by metal posts, there is a house-lined road. On the seaward side are yellow beach huts set above a small sandy cove, all very Victorian- and Edwardian-seaside. A hundred yards down the road, opposite a food store, on the right there is a delightful small park. Beyond the entrance to a small formal garden (where there is a square pool set between rosebeds and four plots in which struggle, more or less successfully, palm saplings), there is a well-mown area leading to the remains of Sandsfoot Castle.

There is not much of Sandsfoot left now but enough to give some idea of how determined Henry VIII was to defend his shores. The castle was built in 1539 and some of the ecclesiastical loot of that year of the Dissolution of the Monasteries went into the military coffers. The ruins are best seen in this little park. I saw the hawthorn in bloom – red, white and pink against the dark background of copper beeches – and the view across to the bulk *couchant* of Portland was Whistlerish in the mauve mist. Multi-coloured small boats shone brightly on the still, early morning waters.

The road past Sandsfoot Castle runs over the brow of a small hill, and opposite the Castle Cove Sailing Club there is a sign to the right indicating a public footpath between some geriatric iron railings, with helpful steps in places, which leads to a bridge over the Sailing Club's private access to Castle Cove. The Path is rough in parts, and some good attempts have been made to pave it with broken bricks and lumps of rubble. There are some well-placed benches from which one can look over to Portland. I thought that the large and careful lettering on one bench was that of the Weymouth local authorities, but I found that it proclaimed 'Dave and Karen'. Where are they now? Are they still on speaking terms, and do they now talk to each other all the time? Do they still remember their signwriting?

Further along, the Path opens out beside a very entertaining brick wall to the left, one of whose courses near the top is set in at an angle, so that the end corners project outwards, and the whole roofed with bricks specially rounded at both ends to let the rain run off. This wall enclosed Bincleaves House, which has now been demolished and its grounds left unprotected by the broken brick walls and some ruined corrugated-iron fences, over which hang disdainfully some tall Scots pines.

This jungly Path emerges on to a greensward overlooked by the Wyke Regis Coast Guard building – small, neat, and fenced within green mesh on its triangular plot. This open space is called Top of Bincleaves, and a man who has lived hereabout all his life told me that what is so often called Undercliff Walk – the path I had just taken – is really called Underbarn Walk, though he could not recall that there had ever been a barn there. He also told me that it was originally intended that the cross-Channel ferries should operate from Bincleaves Groyne, and in the town below a pub was specially built to deal with the expected ferry trade. But in the end the ferry operated from the other side of Weymouth Harbour, and the pub had to rely on local thirst. It is still open.

Bincleaves Groyne and the landing-stage project into the sea below, leaving the North Ship Channel between its extremity and the end of Portland North Eastern Breakwater, thus enclosing Portland Harbour. From the Top of Bincleaves the track leads down past allotments decorated with those fascinating buildings that always sprout on them. I think I shall one day write a book on allotment-building architecture in all its variety, and as a reflection of the personalities of the gardeners.

The Path runs to the right of a tall brick wall into the Nothe Gardens, very sheltered and well maintained. Where the gardens open out there are some public lavatories, and then a green grassy space with many trees, planted mostly in memory of people, and some wooden tables and benches set solidly on concrete bases. You can walk to the end and look at Nothe Fort, a white stone structure set largely below ground level and appearing, at the time of writing, in rather bad shape. But it is being restored and the public may visit it at certain times. Or you can take the right-hand path that leads to a signpost, where one

Nothe Fort and Gardens at Weymouth

arm points left to the Nothe Café and Harbour Ferry, and that is the way to go. Walk towards the Nothe Tavern and turn right in front of Nothe House to go down the steps to the quayside and the rowing-boat ferry operated by Mr Sargent from the beginning of May to the end of September, for a few pence. When the ferry is not in operation, there is a short and pleasant walk along Nothe Parade and into Trinity Street – alongside the harbour all the way – to cross the Harbour at Town Bridge.

The history of Weymouth must inevitably be seen as the successful treatment of Siamese twin towns which, instead of being separated, were fused indivisibly by Act of Parliament, (1 July 1571) into one strong entity incorporating the best attributes of the two former parts. Town Bridge is a good place to begin looking at the history of those two towns on the banks of the river Wey, Weymouth to the south and Melcombe Regis to the north. The Wey rises four miles north, somewhat naturally at Upwey, where George III drank at the much-commercialized spring from the gold cup which is now the Ascot Gold Cup. The wishing-well is in a wooded valley, and from there the Wey has a short and geologically uncomplicated run to the sea through Broadwey, Nottington, Radipole – possibly 'reedy pool' – and Radipole Lake. This is a broad Weymouth backwater, and once it has been crossed by the Embankment Bridge and has negotiated a weir, it becomes The Backwater in name and is divided by the Town Bridge from the Harbour. The Nothe Point is to the south, and the railway station, pier, and esplanade of Weymouth are to the north-east.

The Romans probably had a port here; the Saxons certainly did; and like so many other strategic and profitable places it was for long in the hands of the Church. Because of its geographical position there was much exchange with France, some of it commercial, much of it bellicose. In 1347 the port (in fact the two ports, Weymouth and Melcombe Regis) sent 20 ships and nearly 300 men to the siege of Calais. In July or August of the following year, a more deadly invader than the French struck – the Black Death, the bubonic plague that originated in China and is estimated to have killed nearly 40 million people in the Far and

Weymouth Harbour

Middle East, entered England through Melcombe Regis to claim, eventually, something like 1½ million lives in these islands. Thirty years later, when the inhabitants of the port were said to be attending Mass at Radipole, the French raided and burned both Weymouth and Radipole. A further deadly raid was launched in 1386. Obviously a port that could be sacked without difficulty by the French did not inspire confidence in traders, so they moved their business from Weymouth to Poole where it has prevailed ever since.

It took a fad that became a fashion to establish prosperity in Weymouth. In 1789 King George III was advised to bathe in the sea by his physicians, who suggested Weymouth where the King's brother, the Duke of Gloucester, had a house. The bouts of insanity to which the unfortunate King was subject were due, it is

now known, to porphyria; and it is certain that the sea-bathing in
which he indulged each summer for fifteen years (on occasion to
the strains of 'God Save Great George Our King' from a band
hidden in a neighbouring bathing-machine) did him no harm,
and the relaxed and informal family atmosphere provided some
of the happiest moments in that long and finally most unhappy
life.

One can fairly say that royal bathing did much for Weymouth,
which had been joined, as recorded above, with Melcombe Regis
in 1571 – it was, in fact, the ancient Melcombe Regis that had the
sands, the bay, and the resort we know today. Weymouth's
gratitude to George III for putting the town on the fashionable
map is commemorated in the statue of the King at the southern
end of the Esplanade, a truly astounding monument dedicated in
giant letters by 'the *Grateful* Inhabitants' of Weymouth. It is made
of Coade stone, an artificial cast stone of the late eighteenth and
early nineteenth centuries; it was raised in 1809 and has been
much improved since the end of World War II by being painted
in bright heraldic colours, making what was formerly seen merely
as a monstrosity into something colourful, which you may or may
not like but which, by George, you cannot avoid.

The fine terraces along the front at Weymouth date from the
late eighteenth and the nineteenth centuries; and another
unavoidable monument is the Jubilee Memorial Clock Tower, put
up for Queen Victoria's Golden Jubilee of 1887 and also highly
coloured. A walk along the Front is most rewarding in the depth
of winter, when there is little humanity abroad and one can take
in the un-human-speckled view of the five-mile curving bay which
is unrivalled on the southern coast of England. I have sat on one
of the seafront benches, under polythene-wrapped palm trees,
eating sandwiches in warm January sunshine. At such a time
Weymouth is romantic in a literary sense, with echoes of Jane
Austen and Thomas Hardy, naturally, and faint ones of Thomas
Mann and Marcel Proust as well, perhaps.

But look at the out-of-sight Weymouth too, the Weymouth of
Devenish's brewery (a Victorian red-brick beer temple), the
quays, the berths of the ferries to the Channel Islands and

Cherbourg, the railway that runs unfenced along the quayside in the fashion of *Quai des Brumes* and other old waterfront films. There are a great many pubs and eating-places and bow-windows and nets and fish-boxes in these back areas, seemingly miles away from the busy summer tourist-trade that thrives just around a couple of corners. Wherever you go in Weymouth you end up against some stretch of water, and it is not always easy to know just which it is, inland lake, backwater, the river, harbour, or a bit of the ocean. It is a very stimulating place to walk around and through, and as a pedestrian one quickly senses an enormous advantage over the motorist because Weymouth's one-way mazes seem calculated to keep motorists in motion between double yellow lines until the end of time.

8 Weymouth to Lulworth Cove

Weymouth Esplanade is a mile long and has a pier at either end. For those who prefer not to walk, especially if it is holiday time, there is the Western National Service 417 (end May – middle September) from the King's Statue to Pontin's Holiday Camp, or Services 413/414/415 to Overcombe Corner, from which the Coast Path can be picked up again. Taking the bus avoids $1\frac{3}{4}$ miles of straight and dull road-walking. According to the tide, it is also possible to walk on the shore from the pier at the eastern end of the Promenade all the way to Pontin's at Bowleaze Cove.

Just beyond Overcombe Corner, where the 417 will set you down and where the main road forks to the left, go straight ahead, past the garage, and up the hill to where there is a sign on the left to the Jordan Hill Roman temple. There the Romano-Celtic temple foundations, dating from the first to the fourth centuries AD, are exposed: they were first excavated in 1843, yielding coins, pottery, iron swords and the bases of two Purbeck marble columns. A shaft was discovered in what had been the courtyard, some 15ft deep and filled with the skeletons of ravens, buzzards, crows, starlings, and other birds, arranged carefully and separated by stones or tiles in what was probably some kind of votive offering from pre-Roman times. The site is fenced, but there is free entry through a gate and some information on a notice-board placed there by the Department of the Environment, in whose keeping the temple is.

It is curious to stand by these foundations and look down and over to the startling architecture, Hispanic in inspiration, of the Riviera Hotel set on the eastern bank of the little River Jordan (spelt on some maps Jordon). The road leads down to Jordan's mouth, and then the Coast Path climbs the cliff to seaward of the hotel to come out on open downland among gorse and brambles. Between the path and Redcliff Point there is a jungly undercliff formed by old landslips, somewhat like those seen in the Lyme Regis and Charmouth sections of the Coast Path – with elder, hawthorn, here and there sallow and gorse, willowherb, foxglove, and ragwort splashing colour among the green. The Path goes inland and down to a stile over a fence, beyond which it turns at right-angles to the left for about a hundred yards, before climbing again through gorse and bramble to another dip and a thoughtfully arranged holiday camp of chalets. I had, I thought, read on the map that this was at Shortcake House, and I was prepared to see something out of a Scottish Grimm Brothers' fairy-tale, until I found that it is, in fact, Shortlake House.

The way is signposted past the chalets, and climbs to the top of Black Head, veering inland with collapsed cliffs to seaward. These are thick with undercliff vegetation, dropping to the Black Head Ledges. Looking ahead and below, it seems that some part of the wilderness must be crossed, but keep to seaward of the grassy knoll that is the summit of Black Head, just beyond a pond, and the Path, easier to find in winter than in summer, eventually leads to the bottom of a valley where there is a signpost. Osmington Mills comes into sight, and the Path comes down on the seaward side of the fields into the car-park opposite the Smugglers' Inn. In *The South Devon and Dorset Coast* (1910), Sidney Heath referred to this 'picturesque little cove famed for the quality of its lobsters and prawns, a standing dish at the Picnic Inn [now the Smugglers] being a hot lobster tea, a gastronomic feast that is not so indigestible as it sounds' – that seems to be spoken from the stomach of a good Edwardian trencherman.

Just before you cross the bridge in the pub garden, there is a general shop on the left which is open during roughly the same hours as the pub. There is also a general shop, open in the season, at the Streamside Caravan Park a few hundred yards up the road.

Across the wooden bridge, follow the garden path around the left-hand side of the pub. This leads into a narrow path with a stream on the left running below bridges over to the black wooden Old Coast Guard cottages. A waymarked stile leads to the Path, which rises to the clifftop, passes by some old military installations, and is fenced on the seaward side. Visible at low tide are the rusty remains of the steamer *Minx* which went ashore in 1929. Almost all the dangerous rocks off this part of the coast are called ledges, and between Osmington and Ringstead are Hannah's Ledge, Frenchman's Ledge, Pool Ledge, Bran Ledge (just off Bran Point), Perry Ledge, and Ringstead Ledge.

The Path comes to the present-day Ringstead as a broad track running in front of a line of villas and bungalows, and meets a metalled road running down to the sea. About half a mile before reaching this road, and half a mile inland, is the site of the former village of Ringstead, now low mounds and hummocks grazed by cows and dotted with trees, and lying just to seaward of the secluded Glebe Cottage in whose walls are incorporated the chancel arch of the former Ringstead parish church. It is not known for sure how or why the village disappeared. French raiders, the depredations of pirates, and the Black Death have all been suggested as reasons. It may well be that the plague was the cause, since it could have spread quickly, and perhaps in its initial and most virulent form, from the nearby port of Melcombe Regis.

Turn left into the road for a few yards, to a board on the right that has a plan of the former village and speculation about its fate. Almost opposite, on the seaward side of the public lavatories and a booth that sells most things needed by those spending a day by the sea (including bacon sandwiches and Cornish Ice Cream, both of which I have sampled, though not at the same time), there is a broad unmade track that runs beside more seaside houses where it is difficult to tell the backs from the fronts. The last one in the line has a urinal bowl hung on the wall as a flower urn (urnal?). The road (and the houses to the shore side of it) is called Fisher's

The site of Ringstead medieval village – now just mounds and hummocks in a meadow

Place, after the Miss Fisher who once owned the ground. I have seen it called Fisher's Piece in some guide-books but that is a mistake easily made due to the weathering of the lettering on the board.

At the end of Fisher's Place track is a barrier to prevent motor-cars from going further, and the Path enters the Ringstead Bay National Trust Area at this point. At the end of the first field beyond the barrier, the Path veers left, while ahead there is a thick wood. A path to the right, along the edge of the wood, brings the traveller to an easy, step-assisted route down to the shore of Ringstead Bay, which curves away to the east to where White Nothe juts high at the other end.

The Coast Path follows the landward side of the wood (in which are some cunningly concealed houses), passing over a couple of stiles and wooden footbridges. It then emerges into open pasture and fields, with some cottages and farmhouses, most of them thatched, dotted about on the inland landscape, with a high range of downs behind. The seaward side is Burning Cliff (National Trust) which consists of some chaotic landslips that have given tumbled undercliff in which grow bramble, heather, spur valerian, bladder campion, rushes, spindleberry, and reeds, and which shows a geological variety of blue clay, Greensand, chalk, flint, limestone, marl, Portland stone, Kimmeridge Clay and scrabbled patches of scree. In 1826 there took place a 'pseudovolcanic phenomenon' when oxidation of iron pyrites ignited the oil shales and burning continued below the surface for four years, giving off clouds of dense and evil-smelling smoke, and a name to the cliff. Here too there is a step-aided path down to the shore with warning notices to keep closely to it because of the danger of cliff-falls.

Some two acres of Holworth Cliff slid 30ft in March 1815, complete with a cottage, its garden, and the fisherman and his wife who lived there. In the next three years it all moved several hundred feet out and down towards the sea, and finally came to rest, in the words of an eye-witness, 'as an immense body of cliff bearing on its brow an entire cottage with a garden planted with gooseberry and currant bushes and vegetables, all in a most flourishing condition'. This landslip probably forms part of the present undercliff of Burning Cliff, below which there is secluded and safe swimming in Ringstead Bay.

Just beyond Burning Cliff the Path joins a metalled track, and a short way along to the right is the clapboard church of St Catherine's by the Sea, Holworth. There is nothing remaining of the former village of Holworth, and excavations have shown that there has not been a village here since the fifteenth century. Before that, it was a detached part of Milton Abbas parish some twelve miles to the north, inland. There is a peaceful calm about this tiny church, whose windows overlook the tombstones of its burial ground, which in turn overlooks the sea – most fitting for the many lying there, whose lives and often deaths were closely

The church of St Catherine's by the Sea, at Holworth – a village that vanished in the fifteenth century

bound up with sea-going.

A few yards up the path from the church is a white gate into the grounds of a house surrounded by trees. To the right of the gate, a Coast Path sign points to a tree-shaded path leading out of the trees into an upward-sloping pasture belonging to Sea Barn Farm, which stands at the top and lets both camping and parking space in this pasture, the parking fees being paid into a box at the gate where the 1½-mile-long rough track leads from Owermoigne and the A35 to the top of the cliffs.

The Coast Path continues along the clifftop to White Nothe, White Nore, or White Nose – as Thomas Hardy said it should be called, because in profile the headland resembles the Duke of Wellington's nose. It is possible to climb to the clifftop from the

Mintrice – a Coast Path companion

shore at various points along here, but the excellent *Climbers' Club Guide to Dorset* edited by R.C. White (The Climbers' Club) does not deign to notice it. And rightly, because climbing here is dangerous, and sometimes terrifying. I speak from experience, and I now stay firmly on the clifftop and look down on the broad undercliff where there are ruined wartime buildings, outcrops of rock and patches of scrub. I have seen rabbits, hares, and once a fox, moving around there. Near White Nothe Cottages, a long single-range brick building, there is on the right a passable dry-weather track leading down to the shore.

The cottages are former Coast Guard buildings and, standing here on the crest of White Nothe at nearly 500 ft, they are the highest buildings on the Dorset coast. The Path turns right in

Coast Guard cottages on White Nothe. At 500 ft they are the highest buildings on the Dorset coast

The view eastward from White Nothe – chalk cliffs to Bat's Head, Swyre Head and Lulworth

front of the wall enclosing the cottages, and then passes a now-ruined lookout platform which you can still scale to obtain the very best view – eastward, of the range of chalk cliffs, and westward, over Weymouth Bay to Portland which is seldom out of sight from the Dorset Coast Path.

With pastures and fields inland, the Path along the clifftop is often close to the edge and care is needed, when there is poor visibility, not to stray to the seaward side of the track. To the left of the path are two obelisks for the guidance of shipping. There are some steep gradients along this section, as you take the drop to West Bottom and climb up, to go down again to Middle Bottom and the Warren, and then up again to Bat's Head – and entry into the unique coastal scenery of this eastern section of the Dorset coast. Bat's Head has a rock arch called Bat's Hole which is pierced by the sea at its base and is a kind of histrionic geological warm-up for Durdle Door. Bat's Head presents a vertical chalk buttress to the sea, but from the landward side it is possible to see that it is formed of near-vertical alternating strata of chalk and flint.

Beyond Bat's Head, the Coast Path drops to Scratchy Bottom and then climbs sharply over Swyre Head. The rocks off this stretch of coast are all bovine – the Cow and the Calf off Bat's Head, the Blind Cow off Swyre Head, and the Bull off Scratchy Bottom. These rocks are Purbeck limestone, as is Durdle Door: a natural rock archway formed by the sea, sketched and photographed until it has become a Dorset trademark. Above it is a large holiday-camp, much hidden by trees, and the shingle beach by the Door is crowded through the summer.

The Path climbs sharply again, holding close to the top of the cliffs that shelve less steeply here down to the shore of St Oswald's Bay; and it veers inland a little between Dungy Head and the hill called Hambury Tout, around whose flank it skirts, and descends to seaward of a well-worn track down to the immense Lulworth Cove car-park. At the bottom is a signpost to tell where one has come from, but nothing to indicate where to go next. Beyond the car-park is a café, a souvenir shop, public lavatories, and the Lulworth Cove Hotel over the road where there are tables at which to drink and eat in the pub garden.

Is this how Scratchy Bottom got its name?

Swyre Head and Durdle Door

Durdle Door, with St Oswald's Bay beyond and Dungy Head on the skyline

The path up Hambury Tout from Lulworth Cove – the most intensively used footpath in the whole of Dorset

When ready to get under way again, find Lulworth Cove's one and only street and head towards the sea – but do not rush down without looking. Over the road from the garden of the Lulworth Cove Hotel is a tiny two-storey house, with a painted stone lion's head set into its front wall, called the Doll's House. In the street there is also a little decorative pond, made by damming a stream issuing from the high downs above the cove.

Carry on down the road to the cove, in which there are usually some people messing around in boats. In the off-season they are local fishermen, and during the summer they are visiting anglers and divers. The last building on the left is an ice-cream hut, and beside it is a very steep climb up some wooden steps to the top of the cliff. If the wooden steps are out of action (as they were the last two times I was there), you can take a hard slog over the large pebbles, and climb up the other side of the Bay. But this is not practicable at high tide.

9 Lulworth Cove to Kimmeridge

Lulworth Cove has been formed by the sea breaching the outer limestone cliff to scour out the softer materials of the Wealden Beds and wash them out to sea, leaving a bowl which is almost precisely the shape of a scallop shell, with the narrower end at the sea between high chalk cliffs. When coming out of the car-park watch for a sign to the right to Stair Hole, no part of the Coast Path but a kind of *hors d'oeuvre* to the Cove itself. Here the prehistoric rock-folding can be seen at the eastern end of a miniature cove with a narrow opening and two rock arches, through which the sea frets ceaselessly; it will continue to do so until we are all gone and – should this island itself endure – a breach is made to join Stair Hole to Lulworth Cove.

If you have to take the beach path, look out for the ruins of a limekiln hanging 20 or so feet above the beach. Built of bricks now worn and rounded by sea, air, time, and weather, it clings there – an Ali Baba jar in shape, a cheerful, gigantic, red wasps' nest, built at some time when the level of the cove beach allowed access to it.

Crunching over the stones, one hopes that the pungent smell of

Stair Hole, Lulworth, where the prehistoric rock-folding can clearly be seen

seaweed is therapeutic. There is no specific exit from the beach, and I have tried several. At one point some ruinous steps lead into a path through some low bushes; further on, a steeper, but slippery, path gets to the top quicker. In any case it is quite clear where you are making for: the eastern cliff of the Cove.

At the top is a large stone block engraved 'Pepler's Point', with a metal plate below stating that: 'In memory of Sir George Lionel Pepler, 1882–1959, for fifty years the tenant of Little Bindon, who loved the land of England, worked to the end that it be used for the benefit and enjoyment of its people, and loved Dorset best of all, this promontory is named Pepler's Point.'

Pepler's Point gives a bird's-eye view of what the sea has done to make Lulworth Cove. Treves, author of *Highways and Byways in Dorset* (born in Dorchester and later the surgeon who befriended Joseph Merrick, the tragic 'Elephant Man', and removed Edward VII's troublesome appendix), tells of a girl of eleven who fell 380 ft

from the summit of the landward cliff on 7 September 1892
and escaped without permanent injury. This was not hearsay,
since Treves was called to attend the girl in the Coast Guard
boathouse. There was a strange coincidence, in that when the
news of the fall was brought to him he was reading a book by the
girl's father, who was neither known to Treves nor in Lulworth at
the time.

The next section of the Coast Path runs for some seven miles
through the Ministry of Defence Lulworth Ranges, which for
about thirty years provided a kind of Berlin Wall controversy
(and was nearly as dangerous for those who crossed it by stealth)
in Dorset. After years of doughty fighting against bureaucracy,
with Rodney Legg and the *Dorset Magazine* which he edits
conducting a remorseless Commando campaign of protest, the
MOD in 1974 opened the ranges to the public for most weekends
in the year, at Christmas, at Easter, and from the end of July to
mid-September. The Army accepted the recommendation of the
Nugent Committee on the Defence Lands in that year, that the
public access to the area should be increased. The Army now
issues a pamphlet entitled *Lulworth Range Walks – the Army in
Co-operation with the Public*, giving a map, details of the time the
walks take, the flora and fauna to be observed, and ending with
the exhortation: *Please help preserve this beautiful part of Dorset*.
Here is a splendid example of 'If you can't beat them, join them'.
On the credit side, although the Bindon Range has been a
tank-firing area since 1916, and Heath Range was taken into use
during the Second World War, with the result that much of the
heathland is cruelly scarred, intensive farming, insecticides,
pollution, afforestation in straight-sided blocks of conifers, and
destructive 'development' have all been kept out of the area.

When planning to walk here, always check in the local press, or
by telephone to the Range Officer, RAC Gunnery School (Bindon
Abbey 462721, extension 859) between 0800 and 1700, that the
Path is open. I have always found precise and courteous
information readily given, together with helpful comments on the
state of the path, the weather, visibility, and so on.

Having come to the top of Pepler's Point by one or another

path, you soon reach the range fence and a metal gate. There is a warning notice: 'Metal detectors and hammers prohibited.' (Nothing about sickles, but it is as well to leave those behind also.) A signpost to the left points the way to Little Bindon, where a house, hidden behind giant privet and much other shrubbery, incorporates the remains of parts of the chapel built here by Cistercians (c.1150) as their first foundation for Bindon Abbey, later removed inland to Wool. The path past the house comes out later on to the road from West Lulworth to Lulworth Cove, but it is not part of the Coast Path, which is indicated clearly as going due east along the clifftop. To the right there is a signpost to the Fossil Forest gate, where an explanatory board shows two pictures drawn in colour on perspex by Jane Franklin in 1979, with a caption stating: 'These two pictures show this area as it is now and as it was 120 million years ago when the sea retreated, leaving behind an isolated salt lake. Here lived creatures you see illustrated, the actual trees are not visible but you may see the fossilized "tufa" or growth of algae which surrounded the trunks as that time.'

Some solid steps, concrete at the top and wooden further down, flanked by a stout metal hand-rail, lead to the Fossil Forest, which is like a quarry on a cliff shelf – raw blocks and slices of rock with little vegetation apart from coltsfoot and thrift tucked precariously into corners of powdered limestone that passes for soil. There is something eerie about the Fossil Forest. I have been there when the mist was so thick that it hid the sea below, by sound ever-present; and I have been there in brilliant sunshine; and yet, looking at those stumps tilting like giant stone sea-anemones towards the beholder in almost winsome invitation to the Instamatic, one does on occasion wonder what may lie around the next bluff.

At the very end of the Fossil Forest there is a way of getting to the top of the cliff and the Coast Path again, without going all the way back to labour up the steps. It is unofficial, I have done it several times, and I advise most strongly against it – not because it is unofficial but because, when I got to the top I realized, on coming face to face with a 'Danger – Unexploded Shells, Keep

The Fossil Forest: fossilized tufa which surrounded trees growing here 120 million years ago

Out' sign, that this was stupidly hazardous.

The way through the Range Walks is well marked. Every fifty yards or so a yellow-topped post shows the limits, and triangular red, black, and white-enamelled signs remind one of the danger of unexploded shells. Here and there the path is crossed by wide tracks where tanks come to take up positions on the cliff edge. Along here there is very little gorse (or 'vurze' as it is known in Dorset) but a good deal of fine pink and white clover, knapweed, bird's-foot trefoil, horseshoe vetch, black medick, salad burnet . . . in fact, so many plants flourish luxuriantly because of the absence of weedkillers that hours could be spent classifying what grows in a few square yards.

Rounding Bacon Hole and looking back towards Smugglers' Cave, the Mupe Rocks rise sharply offshore in tilted cones, one of them topped by vegetation, probably sea-holly, thrift, and tenacious grass, and always circled by wheeling gulls – particularly when there is the chance of something being dropped overboard from the small bright-blue boat usually fishing for lobsters along the ledges.

At the point where the Path takes a sharp turn to the north, a flight of steps leads down to the corner of Mupe Bay, where there is good swimming in clear water. When I was last there, a giant notice warned of 'Dangerous chemical containers from the wrecked ship *Aeoleon* [*sic*] *Sky* have been found recently on these beaches. Do not touch any container which you might see but report the find to the police or a range warden.'

On the rise to a stile in the fence there are thick patches of *Campanula rotundifolia* – the true bluebell of Scotland, known as the harebell in England to distinguish it from the wild hyacinth. There is a stiff climb up the southern slope of Bindon Hill, following the curve of Mupe Bay around to the east again. About two-thirds of the way up this gradient, you will find that the Path has been moved inland about a hundred yards – with good reason, because the old path had become dangerously close to the crumbling clifftop. At this point the common sense of the traveller is relied upon, for there is a short and very rudimentary fence across the old path, and the line of yellow-topped stakes leading away up to the left could easily, but pigheadedly, be ignored. At the top of this fairly tough climb a signpost points east to the Coast Path and west to Radar Crossroads, where the radar apparatus monitors boat movements in a sea danger-zone.

From Cockpit Head the Coast Path is a broad turf track, fenced on the landward side. Looking inland over a vast expanse of terrain, from left to right, there are the blue-painted and red-roofed buildings of Lulworth Camp, and a long line of trees with the ruins of Lulworth Castle rising from the middle of them. Built at the beginning of the seventeenth century for the third Viscount Bindon, whose seat was at Bindon Abbey near Wool, it is a four-square, battlemented building with four-storeyed round towers at the corners, all of it built of brick and faced with Purbeck and Portland stone. During the Civil War it was stripped of its lead and iron, and a fire in 1929 completely gutted the building – although from a distance one might believe it still intact. To the right of the castle is the fifteenth-century tower of

The church of St Mary, 1786–7, in the grounds of Lulworth Castle

Lulworth Castle

the parish church of St Andrew. The estate church, which is not visible from the Coast Path, is the 1786–7 Roman Catholic church of St Mary, built by the Roman Catholic Weld family by special permission of George III, who is said to have asked Thomas Weld to make the building as little like a church as possible. It is rather like a pre-Revolutionary French theatre, one mislaid by Louis XV in a Royal Monopoly game, and was described by Fanny Burney as 'a Pantheon in miniature'. Fanny – Madame d'Arblay, and a dedicated weekender in grand houses – was probably flattering her host, because this small church has a warm and yet elegant, intimate atmosphere far removed from the cold and grandiose excesses of Soufflot's Pantheon, still sitting there in Paris and still the source of heated quarrels about who should and who should not be buried there.

For centuries, Lulworth Castle housed the Luttrell Psalter of c. 1340, a record, in more than 300 vellum pages, of contemporary life. It was prepared for Sir Geoffrey Louterell, who is represented in it sitting on a charger with his wife and daughter depicted in the group surrounding him. The Psalter escaped the disastrous fire of 1929, and has been in the British Museum since then. To Lulworth Castle in 1830 came the exiled King of France, Charles X, probably at the suggestion of Cardinal Weld, founder of the Jesuit College at Stonyhurst. Charles X is said to have remarked, uncharitably not to say churlishly, that Lulworth Castle looked uncomfortably like the Bastille! The Weld family now lives in Lulworth Manor, a Queen Anne-style house in red brick, built in the grounds of the Castle.

In the 'gravy-boat' of land between the Coast Path and Lulworth Castle is a criss-cross of tracks, with rusty hulks of ruined tanks dotted about as targets. To the right of this no-man's-land, and in the middle distance, is Maiden Plantation where the lower scrub and saplings are green around the stark grey tops of dead elms.

From this viewpoint the path drops to Arish Mell, where a small stream comes down to the sea from its source in the downs.

Sidney Heath wrote in 1910: 'A grassy walk from [Lulworth Castle] leads to Arish Mill (*sic*) Gap, one of the most striking gullies on the coast where green meadows touch the fringe of golden sand. The scene is often rendered more attractive by groups of cows and sheep. . . . At Arish Mill is the monastery farm where, between 1794 and 1817, Thomas Weld founded a colony of Trappist monks, who remained here until conditions were ripe for their return to France. The neighbourhood of Lulworth is famed for the 'Lulworth Skipper', not a celebrated sea-captain, but a small and rare species of butterfly that has not been found in any other locality.'

These insecticide-free Purbeck clifftop downlands are still very rich in butterflies. I have seen small Skippers and Lulworth Skippers, graylings and the blue butterflies – the Common Blue, the Chalkhill Blue and the Holly Blue. I have, to my shame and certain ignorance, never seen an Adonis Blue. Apart from the Common Blue, the most plentiful butterflies in July on these downs are the Marbled White, graylings and Painted Ladies. I believe that most of the butterflies one sees on the Ranges never venture to the other side of the MOD fences.

Talking of pollution reminds me that the waste from the Atomic Energy Establishment at Winfrith (in Celtic, Winfrith means 'the happy stream') is piped into the sea at Arish Mell, and this knowledge does tend to make one obey the ban on bathing posted there – although I know a man who has swum there for some forty years and shows no post-Hiroshima signs on his shining bronzed face and body. Just the same, obey the rules and keep out, because ONE NEVER KNOWS – 'Do one?' as Fats Waller had it.

The Path is still broad but is badly worn on the climb from Arish Mell, and in wet weather it can be a slimy and treacherous chalk porridge. But in summer the path is bordered with flowers, the blue of wild chicory, the deeper blue of viper's bugloss, yellow sea-poppies and ragwort. The Path climbs steadily above Holcombe Vale to the top of Ring's Hill which is crowned by Flower's Barrow, an Iron Age hill-fort dating from around the fourth century BC, now covering some 15 acres but with much of its earlier acreage lost to the sea at Worbarrow Bay. From Flower's Barrow there are views, when the weather is right, of Worbarrow Bay, Worbarrow Tout (which sits, triangular and like a miniature Gibraltar, off the coast) and, inland and eastwards, Tyneham Gwyle. There is a footpath from Flower's Barrow to the Creech Hill road and the car-park on Whiteway Hill – this is a fine walk, but if you are on the Coast Path there is a right turn down to the root of Worbarrow, where few walkers can resist exploring. Another path from here goes inland for just over a mile along Tyneham Gwyle to Tyneham village.

The story of Tyneham has been told many times, and controversy over its fate still exists. I wrote in *Dorset Villages*:

During World War II the Army took over a vast area of Purbeck for training purposes, evacuating 255 people from their homes with the promise that they would be allowed to return when the war ended. But those exiles who survive are still exiles, and about a thousand acres, from $5\frac{1}{2}$ miles of coastline between Lulworth and Brandy Bay and extending five miles northwards, is still crawled over by tanks and fired over by artillery. For nearly thirty years a campaign was waged to get the Army out, or at least to get the area opened up occasionally to the public. In 1974 Lord Nugent's Defence Lands Committee report was published and on the same day a public trust was founded, Friends of Tyneham Limited . . . 'ready to step in when the ten square miles of the Dorset coastal army ranges are released'. Meanwhile, awaiting that release, funds are being raised towards projects to protect Dorset's most outstanding wildlife refuge and to help restore Tyneham's battered historic buildings.

The church has now been leased to the Army for twenty-one years (!) from 1977 as a museum . . . The first time I saw Tyneham was in 1943 after scrambling ashore from a bumpy and puke-streaked landing-craft. I can remember little about this exercise or why we parachutists were involved in a mock-up of a seaborne invasion. I recall sleeping on the floor of an empty house near the church, which I have not been able

The ruins of Tyneham village, taken over by the Army during World War II

to identify on subsequent visits, but the old concrete telephone kiosk, of a style that was even then very rare, still exists.

In the church museum Visitors' Book is the comment: 'A good museum, but how sad.' There is a display of photographs of Tyneham when it was a real village, with the manor house that was begun in 1567, completed in 1583, and is now demolished. The village street is a line of ruins with 'Keep Out' notices everywhere, a dead village with the Army doing its best to gloss over the artillery-target past by building a village pond and a 1977 Jubilee flower garden, and by having an often hard-pressed young soldier in civilian clothes in attendance to answer questions. I remember a bearded man of about thirty-five saying to his wife and children in a Birmingham accent, 'It's too sad, too awful. I wish I'd never brought you here.'

Well, it may be 'too sad' to make the detour to Tyneham, yet it should be seen and reflected upon.

Forgetting the detour to Tyneham, the Coast Path climbs steadily, from the disused Coast Guard station at Worbarrow to the top of Gold Down, between barbed-wire fences, revealing a long shorescape of limestone cliffs above Wagon Rock (how did this name from the Dakota plains get here?) and the awesome Gad Cliff where there is some of the wildest cliff scenery in Dorset. The Path climbs to 550 ft above sea level from here to the top of Tyneham Gap, where there is a signpost at a fork, the right-hand arm pointing to the Coast Path, the other marking the way inland to Kimmeridge village. The Path descends around the line of Brandy Bay and Hobarrow Bay, and follows the contour of Broad Bench to seaward of the disused oil well on one of the Kimmeridge shale 'shelves' along this part of the coast. Just beyond here is the intriguingly named, and perhaps sinister, Charnel Cove.

From here on the Path runs to seaward of cultivated fields, and comes out of the Range Walks at the point where the coast begins to bend inwards at the start of Kimmeridge Bay. Just on the far side of the gate out of the Range is the famous Nodding Donkey oil well that nodded Britain into the oil age. Painted green, it is well camouflaged and not a blot on the landscape but a simple-looking piece of machinery with the donkey's head nodding up and down and drawing a fragile-looking steel cable out of the earth, while the rest of the construction, boldly marked Legrand, purrs along quietly.

10 Kimmeridge to Swanage

Walk down the metalled road from the oil well, and where it makes a right-angle bend to the left go over the stile and alongside the gardens of the row of cottages (built at one of the many times when Kimmeridge was thought to have an industrial future). Continue down to the wooden bridge over a stream which looks on the inland side to be a bubbling burn but which to seaward becomes a sullen and stagnant pool; go up the steps and

Oil well 'nodding donkey' pump, Kimmeridge Bay: the first onshore well in Britain, drilled in 1959

into the car-park (lavatories nearby) where there is an information board giving a detailed description of sea vegetation here at Gaulter Gap.

The shore is uninviting here because of the predominant greyish colour of both sand and rocks: the Kimmeridge shale colour. But this is a popular part of the coast for divers, and throughout the summer cars and vans with international markings, gas cylinders, wet suits set out to dry, and brawny chaps and girls sunning themselves above the surface, are much in evidence.

Kimmeridge has a long industrial history, almost all of it abortive. The Kimmeridge clay hereabouts is rich in fossils and one of them, *Pliosaurus grandis*, now displays its seven-foot-long head in Dorchester Museum. This clay has layers of bituminous shale, the hardest of which is called blackstone or Kimmeridge Coal. In prehistoric times, and during the Roman Occupation, the blackstone was fashioned into ornaments; the discs that were later called 'coal money' were waste material from the rings and amulets turned on primitive lathes. The Romans also made salt here, and in the early seventeenth century Sir William Clavell boiled seawater to make salt, using the shale as fuel. Clavell also tried his hand at making alum, glass, and at building Kimmeridge into a port: stone blocks from his pier can still be seen on the east side of Kimmeridge Bay. But all failed, and poor old Clavell spent time in prison before dying in 1644.

In 1847 there was another attempt to make money out of the oil-bearing shale, and an Act of Parliament of that year allowed tramways, inclined planes, and causeways to be built to get the shale out for transport to Weymouth, where naphtha, dyes, pitch, and varnish were extracted from it. There was even a plan to light the streets of Paris with gas refined from the shale-oil, but it reeked so strongly of sulphur that the project was abandoned. Kimmeridge eventually came into its industrial own in 1959 with the nodding donkey: the first onshore oil well in the United Kingdom. Rodney Legg gives a very interesting and amusing account of Kimmeridge and the attempts to make it part of England's Industrial Revolution in his book *Purbeck Island*.

Cross the field, which is muddy in winter and covered with motor-cars in summer, to where a Coast Path sign points the way to a flight of steps and a wooden bridge over another narrow stream flowing to the sea between grey shale walls. The Path comes out on to a little quay, and over to the left there is a flight of steps. I once, out of curiosity, counted 52 after hearing a small boy and his grandmother argue as to whether there were 85 or 86. Maybe one or the other was right, as I never could count anyway. But however many there are of them, they lead to the top of Hen Cliff and Clavel's Tower. (I do not know why there is one 'l' in here when there are two in the family name, but the tower has only one.)

The man who had this built was really called the Reverend John Richards, but he took the name Clavell when he inherited

Clavel Tower, Kimmeridge: built as an observatory, now a romantic folly

Smedmore estate in 1817. He had the tower built (c.1820) as an observatory, and it is now a romantic folly, the stucco fallen away to reveal the workaday brick beneath, with a Tuscan colonnade around the ground storey and mock machicolation and a parapet around the top. It is obviously extremely unsafe and is protected by a half-hearted barbed-wire fence which seems less to keep vandals out than to preserve the fine sea-cabbage and mallow growing inside it.

The Coast Path carries on, high above the Kimmeridge Ledges that splay out into the sea. Cultivated fields lie to landward and there is easy going over Cuddle – 'caudle' is a miner's term for mud. Clavell's Hard was once joined by tramways to the old shale workings, and traces of them can still be seen in the inland fields.

Rounding Rope Lake Point – a rope lake is a waterfall – a strong smell of seaweed rises from the Kimmeridge Ledges, and from here the whole bay stands clear to St Aldhelm's Point, which many locals call St Alban's Head.

Inland is a landscape of rolling hills, the highest of them the 670-ft Swyre Head, to which there is a footpath (about a mile in length) from the Coast Path. The Path has a stretch of open clifftop walking before a steep drop brings you to the wooded valley of South Gwyle. This is the seaward path of a long and very private stretch of woods, with a dairy farm and, beyond two artificial lakes, Encombe House, which is the seat of the Earls of Eldon. At Egmont Bight – which sounds like Beethoven arranged by one of those breezily nautical twentieth-century English composers – a stream breaks from the trees to fall through a stone conduit in a cascade to the sea below, at yet another Freshwater.

The Path climbs steeply through, and beyond, bushes – steps in places help along the climb up here unless cliff falls have destroyed them – to come out on the open clifftop over Houns-tout, with its jungly undercliff falling in scrubby shelves down to the sea at Egmont Point. To the right is a view over the wooded valley of Encombe showing the degree of isolation achieved in the eighteenth and nineteenth centuries. In a much-quoted sentence of Treves, it is said that the owner closed the grounds at the beginning of this century 'owing to the atrocious conduct of the trippers'.

On top of Houns-tout a path goes 1½ miles inland to the village of Kingston and the road to Corfe Castle. From the churchyard in Kingston there is the best sight of Corfe Castle, showing how strategically well placed it was on its mound between two hills. The church of St James, built by the third Earl of Eldon between 1873 and 1880 to replace the old church (built only in 1833), is a masterpiece of Victorian Gothic constructed in local Purbeck stone.

On Houns-tout there is a slab of Purbeck stone and a stile where the Coast Path begins to descend; gently at first, and then steeply by a flight of steps (often in a ruinous state), to Chapman's Pool, a secluded cove of grey cliffs with a pebble beach and an abundance of fossils. Because of the very dangerous cliffs and frequent rock-falls, Chapman's Pool at the time of writing is closed to the public, who can only come near to the cliffs by a toll

road. Negotiating Chapman's Pool on foot is now largely a matter
of common sense. A bridge over a narrow stream, where there is
a stone marker bearing the acorn, leads into a rocky and
overgrown little valley, from which you head for the shore and
some old and battered boat-houses above the beach. If the tide is
out, the simplest route is by the shore until you reach the point
where it is easiest to move inland to pick up the original Path,
before the cliffs rise too precipitously again. If the state of the tide
precludes this route, try to follow the original path, which runs
below the sheer cliffs through the undercliff. There used to be
yellow-topped stakes along it, but I did not notice any remaining
the last time I walked there. In wet weather this path is
treacherous, and when it is dried out in summer, traces of other
and wetter seasons are evident in the bits of wood, stones, crushed

Corfe Castle

furze and scuffed branches that have been deposited in the worst of the muddy hollows. It is a broken-up landscape of stunted hawthorn, bramble thickets, beds of purple loosestrife.

This path runs below Emmett's Hill, towering limestone bluffs with flat tops – real Indian country in which the ambush awaits the covered wagon-train. Whether you take the shore or the rudimentary path, it becomes obvious that a great flight of steps is intended to help the walker up the next rise. At the foot of the steps a signpost shows the path inland along a valley to Renscombe Farm (¾ mile) and to the village of Worth Matravers (¼ mile), and the Coast Path distances of 3¾ miles back to Kimmeridge, and 1 mile east to St Aldhelm's Head. The first part of the eastward trail is more than 200 steps.

At the top, St Aldhelm's Chapel, Coast Guard buildings, and cottages stand out against the sky. The summit is a fairly level plateau, broken here and there by Purbeck stone quarries but for the most part cultivated fields, bright with poppies, mallow, camomile, yarrow in every shade from chalky white through pale pink to raspberry-and-cream, and with the rich red of docks glowing among the ripening corn. This summit is 350 ft above the sea, and the cliffs fall abruptly to a 'race' like that off Portland Bill.

There have been many shipwrecks off the Head and they provoke thoughts about St Aldhelm's chapel. *Was* it a Chapel – if so why is it not orientated, and why are there no traces of either altar or piscina? It may have served a dual purpose as chapel and as guide to shipping, perhaps the latter being its more important function. It was built in the late twelfth century, square and with walls more than 3ft thick. Inside, the floor measures roughly 25ft by 25ft, with a central pier and four rib vaults. There is a round-arched Norman doorway in the north-west side and one deep, narrow, lancet window below a round arch. Another window on the west side has been blocked up. If the round turret on the roof was indeed a cresset in which a fire was lit as a guide to shipping, the monk in charge presumably reached it by ladder, because there is no apparent way of doing so from within the chapel.

St Aldhelm's Chapel, St Aldhelm's Head. The cresset on the roof held a fire to guide sailors

A notice outside the chapel declares that: 'You are now at St Aldhelm's Head, 350ft above sea level. The trading vessel *Halsewell* struck rocks near this headland just over 200 years ago. Passengers and crew struggled to reach the cliffs but many failed. Several went down with the ship, including the captain and his daughters. Survivors were helped to safety by quarrymen but 168 people still perished.'

The white-painted Coast Guard lookout building is perched on the very edge of the cliff and in front of it is a gigantic blue board, lettered in white 'H.M. Coast Guard St Aldhelm's Head', which must be visible from many miles out to sea. Beside the building is a stone Coast Path marker bearing the acorn and pointing west to Chapman's Pool (1¼ miles) and east to Winspit (1½ miles). Nearby a wooden board warns: 'Coast Path to Chapman's Pool closed. Access to the Pool from the toll road above has been closed since 1977. Dorset County Council.' But since that notice was put there I have walked this section of the Coast Path in both directions and, instead of the shorewalking, one can take the inside of the wire fence that borders the presently perilous path along the edge of cultivated fields and pastures on the top of Emmett's Hill. At the western end it is again a question of common sense to find one's way down to Chapman's Pool and take the path up the steps on the other side. The South West Way Association will gladly send, on receipt of a stamped self-addressed envelope, information on the right-of-way position and the condition of the path at any particular moment, to those intending to walk there.

From the Coast Guard lookout the Path follows the cliff edge, giving fine walking for about a mile on the cliffside of a barbed-wire fence. The vegetation along here is again typical of the chalk – mallow, scabious, viper's bugloss, and a sprinkling of sea-cabbage and sea-beet. At one point the path veers inland around a tiny bay that looks as if it had been cut out of the coastline with a giant apple-corer. It is vertiginous near the edge, but if you creep to it gingerly, as I do, and have good eyesight, or carry a monocular or field-glasses, you may distinguish, among the ubiquitous herring gulls, razorbills, kittiwakes, fulmars and guillemots.

Beyond the down called West Man, the Path drops gradually to the narrow combe of Winspit Bottom running between it and East Man on the other side, from Worth Matravers a mile inland, down to Winspit and the limestone quarries that were worked for centuries right up until the end of the Second World War. On the sides of the combe are traces of strip lynchets, and the mouth of the combe has been opened out and broken up by the quarries, which present sheer rock-faces, caves made by the men in extracting the rock, and the ruins of quarry buildings. The great blocks of stone used to be lowered by derricks or 'whims' into barges moored – dangerously when the sea was rough – at the foot of the cliffs, ready to take the stone around Durlston Head and Peveril Point to Swanage.

A mile inland, Worth Matravers is a village built of the stone from which its inhabitants earned their living. The pub, the Square and Compass, is named after stonecutters' implements, and is so small and low-ceilinged that it is like a quarrymen's cave perched on its grassy triangle. Worth's church is dedicated to the patron saint of sailors, St Nicholas of Myra; it is Norman with traces of Saxon, and has a fine pyramidal tower of 1869. Buried in the churchyard is Benjamin Jesty who introduced smallpox vaccination by inoculating with cowpox members of his own family in 1774.

Three-quarters of a mile along the coast from East Man is the site of another abandoned quarry – Seacombe – from which another footpath, through Seacombe Bottom, leads to Worth Matravers. At Seacombe the different layers of Portland stone stand out clearly, and it is here that the Under Freestone, the choice building stone, lay in its thickest seam of nine feet and was extracted in galleries whose roofs were supported by square columns of stone left for that purpose as the quarrying proceeded underground. One can get down to the sea at Seacombe, and there is good swimming on calm days in the deep water where the barges used to moor.

Half a mile from Seacombe is Hedbury Quarry, so marked on the OS maps but known to local people and all those who pass that way as Cannon Cove because of the gun mounted there in the Napoleonic Wars, rediscovered among the rubble and remounted in the 1970s. The Path continues high along the clifftop, with splendid views both ahead and inland over the wide pastures and fields, for half a mile to the next disused quarry, Dancing Ledge. The Under Freestone was quarried from Dancing Ledge by underground workings, leaving caves and a level terrace over which, it is said, the waves seem to dance at high tide. Well . . . the name could easily have come from some more fanciful idea of it being a place suitable for waltz or polka. At the western edge of the ledge are dressed stone blocks with grooves left in them by the wedges, and running towards the cliff-edge are marks made by the trolleys that took the stone to the barges. In 1910 an enterprising schoolmaster had a swimming-pool drilled in the flat surface of the Ledge for his boys, the pool being filled with sea-water at high tide.

From Dancing Ledge the Path stays close to the clifftop (which for the next two miles is rougher and more broken, with stone rubble and outcrops of rock, pastureland and some scrub on the landward side), crossing stone walls by stiles. To seaward there are tangles of hawthorn, sallow, and bramble, and only one significant cove breaks the line of the cliffs: Blacker's Hole. A couple of hundred yards along from Blacker's Hole stand a pair of shipping markers that are matched by another pair one nautical mile (6,080ft) to the east. There is a small National Trust enclave called Belle Vue which ends at a sign pointing to Dancing Ledge (1¾ miles) and to Durlston immediately ahead. Here the Coast Path enters Dorset County Council's Durlston Country Park, 261 acres made into a park in 1973, a most successful effort to turn this part of an area of outstanding natural beauty (usually written with capital letters) into a natural and un-park-like space, with walks and nature trails running through it.

On Anvil Point, which gets its name from an anvil-shaped rock at sea-level below, stands a lighthouse, a sturdy no-nonsense building of 1881, with the keeper's cottage within high walls, all remaining today just as when it was built. Beyond the lighthouse stands the second pair of lattice-metal nautical mileposts, the requisite 6,080ft beyond those passed earlier along the Path, and marking of a measured mile for trials and races out at sea.

The path continues across a dry valley to the tunnel entrance to Tilly Whim Caves, relics of quarrying which were popular with visitors until, due to the danger of falling rock, they were closed to the public in 1977. Dorset County Council is still considering whether it will be possible to reopen the caves.

The Path now has a stone wall on its seaward side and leads through tamarisk and ilex, which in summer give a Mediterranean appearance and scent – particularly when the sun turns the sea to deep blue beyond the golden samphire. The Path doubles back inland at Durlston Head just beyond the Great Globe, a forty-ton replica of the world, made at Greenwich in fifteen segments in 1887. The Globe was commissioned and set

The Great Globe, at Swanage. In the background is Durlston Castle

Durlston Castle – George Burt's nineteenth-century pleasure dome, now a cafeteria

up by George Burt, a stone-merchant who, with his uncle John Mowlem, decorated nineteenth-century Swanage by bringing back as ballast from London (having discharged their loads of Purbeck stone) cast-iron posts and bollards, many marked with the names of London boroughs and iron-founders. They imported much, much more, including the 1668 Portland stone façade from Mercers' Hall, which can now be seen above the door of Swanage Town Hall.

Beyond the Great Globe, and the cannon-posts that surround it, may be seen the amazing turrets of George Burt's Durlston Castle, its walls engraved with improving geographical information about that wonderful world of 1890. Intended as a restaurant, it has merely undergone a sea-change of the times and is now a cafeteria: when the hour is right, or the wind in a good quarter (facts not inscribed on the walls of George Burt's mighty pleasure dome), the bar is open too, only a couple of hundred yards from the Coast Path. Architecturally, the Castle was described by Treves as having the 'features of a refreshment buffet, a tram terminus and a Norman keep'.

1 Swanage

Follow the Path inland from the Castle, and a few yards between trees brings you out at the Durlston Country Park car-park, where there is an information centre during the summer season. Turn right along the broad woodland path that follows the gentle curve of Durlston Bay, across which there is a fine view from here, and about half a mile from the Castle a path leads down to the beach. The Coast Path here goes up some steps past tall blocks of flats. Turn right at the top of the steps into a lane that comes out almost immediately on to the open downland and Peveril Point. From the Point there is a panorama of the town of Swanage, the front, Swanage Bay, and Ballard Point at the northern extremity of the bay, where the coast straightens out into a NNE line to the Foreland or Handfast Point.

Carry on round Peveril Point past the Coast Guard lookout and the Lifeboat House, open to the public 0900-1700 weekdays. There are two piers, dating from 1859 and 1896, the former built for the shipping-out of stone, and no longer in use; the second an unpretentious jetty 1,400ft in length, built almost alongside the first. Then comes one of those unique features of Swanage, a clockless clock-tower that began life at the Southwark end of London Bridge in 1854 as a memorial to the Duke of Wellington but which was taken in 1868, with many more bits of London, to Swanage – often described as 'Old London by the Sea'!

Swanage can be walked through and around in about an hour. Apart from packing into Swanage artifacts from old London, Burt built for himself a mansion called Purbeck House which incorporated a tower faced with granite chips from the Albert Memorial. Had there been enough of them, I am sure that Burt would have had Albert chips with everything. Pre-Burt, and on a much smaller scale, is the windowless lock-up at the back of the Town Hall, 'erected for the prevention of vice and immorality by the Friends of Religion and Good Order, 1803'. Post-Burt is the twelve-sided glass, steel and Purbeck stone Public Library of 1965. And it may be the time of day to look for the youth hostel which, after you have crossed the High Street from the Public Library, is just a short walk down Mount Pleasant Lane on the corner of Cluny Crescent (tel. 2113).

The Coast Path follows the Parade and Shore Road along the seafront, passing the Mowlem Theatre (how many black-face singers tried their luck with 'How I love yer, my dear old Swanage'?) and the granite column inscribed 'In commemoration of a great Naval battle fought with the Danes in Swanage Bay by Alfred the Great AD 877' and topped bizarrely with three cannon balls from the Crimean War!

At low tide it is possible to walk on the beach from the Coast Guard building at Peveril Point, passing below the terrace of the Hotel Grosvenor, to just past the pier. Here the official Coast Path takes a break to let the walker find his own way, the easiest thing on earth, through Swanage. On the beach, I find the regular and monotonous interruption by groynes and the occasional skirmish with a vagrant and dislocated deck-chair rather boring. More amusing, and less of a pebbly slog, is Shore Road – which is really the Front – past the smells of cooking, crazy golf, the Tourist Information Centre, public conveniences, bathing huts and all the varied architectural and civic jumble to be expected from a fishing village that became a stone-exporting port and later a Victorian holiday resort. It was nourished by the railway (which killed the stone trade from the quay), which came in 1885 as a branch line from Wareham, and was closed in 1972.

2 Swanage to Studland and South Haven Point

The beach route ends just beyond the last wooden breakwater where a footpath leads beside a small stream up the cliff to the Coast Path. If tide and preference indicate the inland route, which is longer but easier, then walk to the end of the Front or Shore Road that finishes at a car-park and a café called the Ocean Swell. The road forks off inland under the name of Ulwell Road and leads eastward to what is somewhat grandly called New Swanage and eventually to Studland and the ferry, or westward to Corfe Castle. Walk about half a mile up Ulwell Road and just past Victoria Road, and leading off to the right opposite Swanage Football ground, is All Saints Church. Keep on up the hill to the right of the church, ignore Ballard Road, and take the next turning to the right, Ballard Way, at the end of which is a public footpath through the Ballard Estate of bungalows and gardens of prizeworthy luxuriance.

Turn left when you come to a field and see the Coast Path sign. A flight of steps goes down to the beach; follow them as far as the footbridge, and then take the steps going up to the path on the clifftop. The going in high summer is enclosed by bracken and brambles until the top of Ballard Cliff, on the seaward side of the National Trust's Studland Hill and of Ballard Down, which is crossed by a footpath to Studland village. The Coast Path goes due east out to, and around, Ballard Point but there is a footpath cutting across the Point: I mention this because, while the Path to the Point itself should not be missed, there is a triangulation point on the footpath from which there is a magnificent view back over Swanage Bay and ahead over Studland Bay and Poole Bay.

The Dorset cliffs from here on are chalk, and from the sheer white face of Ballard Point to Handfast Point (also called the

Foreland) they make a dramatic panorama that comes into view as the path drops gently across the down called Old Nick's Ground – which is exorcized by the cave below called Parson's Barn. Unlike any cliffscape seen on the way from Plymouth, the edge of the land here seems to have been clipped by worn and uneven pinking shears to make a fringe of chalk banded with black flint, a fringe detached at Handfast Point into Old Harry Rocks. (Old Harry was, of course, the Devil.) This clifftop, where the Purbeck Hills reach the sea, was left to the National Trust in 1981 by Henry Bankes, along with Corfe Castle and the rest of the 25 square miles of Dorset which had been in his family since before the Civil War.

There is some confusion about Old Harry and his family. Harry's Wife suffered severe storm damage in 1896 and only a stump of the stack remains while Harry himself is said to have succumbed before 1905, when C.G. Harper's *The Dorset Coast* referred to Harry having been at last 'flung down'. The names do not matter much, but there is an incestuous note to all this in that the OS maps mark Old Harry and Old Harry's Wife while other records call the slender stack 'Old Harry's Daughter'. Whoever she is, some of her is still there – but for how long? – just beyond the larger block which is either Old Harry or No Man's Land, always surrounded and covered by gulls, cormorants and a variety of other sea-birds. It is separated from the mainland by a gap forced by the sea in the winter of 1920–1 and now known as St Lucas Leap – not named for an electrified saint, but for a greyhound that leapt over the edge in pursuit of a hare. I have never learned what happened to the hare.

In clear weather the Needles stand out against the coast of the Isle of Wight, the remaining stacks of the far end of a continuous chalk bridge that linked Wight to the mainland until the sea brought about its collapse 8,000–10,000 years ago. Eastward, the glassy towers of Bournemouth gleam high above the curve of Poole Bay: the Bay ends in the Beerpan Rocks off lager-coloured Hengistbury Head, behind which Christchurch Harbour lies sheltered from the south-west gales. From a balcony on the top floor of the highest of these high-rise buildings in Bournemouth,

I scanned the whole of the bay, from Durlston Head to
Hengistbury Head, through binoculars on a bright clear day. My
host on that occasion was Wilfred Beeching, who founded and
presented to Bournemouth the fascinating Typewriter Museum
which presents a unique veteran and vintage collection and is
open to the public (weekdays, including Saturday, 0900–1700,
tel: Bournemouth 21009).

From Handfast Point the Coast Path turns west, veering slightly
southwards, for a mile along the north-facing stretch of coast,
starting along the seaward edge of Studland Wood – so named,
although distant from the village – and running above the little
coves and inlets of Studland Bay along a well-trodden farm track,
and through a corner of Warren Wood. Follow this broad track
until it meets the road, and turn right up the hill, past the Bankes
Arms Hotel on the left and the Manor House Hotel on the right.
The next turning to the right leads past a car-park to the beach,
where a Coast Path sign points to the sand dunes in a general
northerly direction. But to carry straight on there is to miss one of
the prettiest villages in Dorset, and in the whole of England.
Specific directions are difficult, but the village is so small that a
little wandering around will soon bring into sight everything that
is to be seen.

The church, dedicated like so many along this coast to St
Nicholas of Myra, is set among ancient yews, and has a
pre-Conquest chancel and central tower, with a nave which was
rebuilt in the twelfth century. The church may have been raised
on the site of an even earlier building that could have been a
pre-Christian temple. The corbel is decorated with grotesque
carvings of human faces, animals, and symbols that seem to reach
back through the Middle Ages to pre-Christianity.

A thick slice of what is in comparison modern history are the
tombstones of Sergeant John Lawrence of the 40th Regiment of
Foot (who lies a few yards from the church door and who served
in South America and Spain and 'fought in the glorious battle of
Waterloo') and of his wife, Clotilde Clairet of St Germain-en-
Laye, near Paris. Lawrence had run away from the bullying
builder to whom he was apprenticed in 1804, and returned to

St Nicholas of Myra, Studland: one of the most complete Norman village churches

Gargoyles at the church of St Nicholas, Studland

Studland when his military service was ended to run a pub until his death in 1869 – a great loss to bar-room historians, I imagine.

Studland beach is a geological meeting-place. In visual terms, the white of the chalk (from Ballard Cliff, around the shoulder of Handfast Point, to where the coast takes a northern turn again just before Studland) is topped by light-coloured sands and clays. Further on, there is dark-brown ironstone, and further north still along the beach the yellow sands and clays are stained red with ferric-oxide. Redend Point is a headland of iron-hardened sandstone with an 'apron' sandstone ledge and caves on either side of the Point. The reds and yellows here have their counterpart in Alum Bay in the Isle of Wight recalling, as do the Needles and Old Harry Rocks, the land bridge that used to be. At low tide it is possible to round Redend Point by the beach, but whether you do this or come out of the village of Studland, the last phase of the South-West Coast Path begins with little change of scenery.

But what scenery! More than three miles of broad beach of fine pale sand, from the whole length of which there is safe swimming, is bordered on the landward side by sand-dunes forming the shoreline-edge of a 400-acre nature reserve, a wonderful wilderness of marram and lyme grass, giving way to heather and bog-myrtle, birch, sallow, and alder. A board put up by the Nature Conservancy Council shows the area of the Reserve, which is bordered by Poole Harbour to the west and Shell Bay to the east, and it explains:

> This Reserve is made up of dunes, heathland, woodland, marsh and a freshwater lake (Little Sea) which is an important place for ducks in the winter. It is especially rich in dragonflies and contains all six kinds of British reptiles. There is a wide variety of plants and animals here including some rarities. The Reserve is leased from the Kingston Lacy and Corfe Castle Estate by the Nature Conservancy Council. . . . [In fact, since 1981 it has been owned by the National Trust] . . . Please help to protect this reserve, avoid disturbing plants and animals. A permit is required for specimen collection. Please do not leave

litter. Keep dogs under control. Do not disturb scientific equipment. Because of the extreme fire-risk, avoid lighting fires and take great care to put out cigarettes. Warning, there is still a possibility of finding unexploded missiles from the Second World War. Do not touch any metal objects as they may explode. Please report them to the police. Further information about the Reserve and Nature Trails can be obtained from the Warden, Mr. R.J. Cox, 33 Queens Road, Swanage (tel. Swanage 3453) and the National Nature Reserves established by the Nature Conservancy Council to safeguard areas of outstanding importance for nature conservation.

The Nature Reserve covers about 1,500 acres and the notice was placed there on 13 June 1977. The Reserve limits are marked by white concrete milk churns – that is what they resemble to anyone who can remember what churns look like – and they follow the shore-line up to Number 13, where an arrow points inland.

About midway between Studland and South Haven Point there is a stretch of beach that seems subject to a tacit understanding that it shall be a playground of naturists. They do not bother the fully or partly dressed, and seem not to be objects of either curiosity or harassment by anyone.

Soon the orange cliffs and tall towers of Bournemouth come into sight; out to sea, the white cliffs of the Isle of Wight are background to large vessels passing to and from Poole Harbour. Around a shoulder of shore, Studland Bay becomes Shell Bay, named for the variety of shells cast up by the tides – oyster, cockle, mussel, razor, periwinkle, tellin, pandora, and cuttlebone, as well as marine animals' egg-cases, such as the black, four-pointed 'mermaids' purses' – the egg-cases of the skate and ray families – and the pale-coloured leathery cases of the common whelk.

Shell Bay ends at South Haven Point at the entrance to Poole Harbour, and the South West Peninsula Path ends – or begins – here. There is little here apart from some well tucked-away public lavatories, a shop, a boatbuilding yard, a car-park and many

notices forbidding parking anywhere along the sides of the road –
but thousands of motorists do so regularly – and stating where
you should get your car in line for the ferry. Walkers board the
ferry, which crosses every twenty minutes (except for about a
fortnight in November), by walking along a raised and railed-off
metal pathway, safe from the traffic.

The Hants and Dorset bus service No 147 leaves Shell Bay for
Swanage at ten minutes past the hour, and crosses to the
Bournemouth side at half-past the hour. If you are walking from
east to west, look carefully, at the left-hand side of the road as you
leave the ferry, for the Coast Path signpost which is set on a sandy
bank and held there by marram grass. This is placed just before
the first building on the left, and on the other side of the dune are
the sands of Shell Bay, so that within minutes of leaving the ferry

Shell Bay, Dorset – the end (or the beginning) of the Coast Path

one is on the Coast Path – very different from starting in the west and getting up and out of Plymouth.

There is a clear view of the Haven Hotel and the suburbs leading to Bournemouth on the other side and of the wooded Brownsea Island in Poole Harbour stretching away inland. South of Brownsea lies Furzey Island, and just below Furzey is even smaller Green Island, where potters still work with the clay they dig there as has been done since before the Romans. The buildings of Poole and Hamworthy seem to press to the rim of the Harbour. But over there is another world from the South West Way, much more than just a ferry-ride away.

Alternative High-Level Inland Route

West Bexington to Osmington Mills

Introduction

The Weymouth conurbation is the only part of the Dorset Coast Path that is outside the Dorset Area of Outstanding Natural Beauty. An alternative high-level route of about 17 miles avoids Weymouth and stays in the Natural Beauty Area throughout its entire length. However, a Coast Path is expected to follow the coast and this alternative path does not: at one point it is 8 miles from the sea. Philip Carter, Secretary of the South West Way Association, told me that there appears to be little interest in the route – 'We have not had a single enquiry about it in some seven years of correspondence about practically everywhere else on the path.'

So who is likely to take it, and what is to be said for doing so? First, obviously, are those Coast Path travellers who wish to avoid the Weymouth area in the height of the holiday season. Secondly, those already familiar with the regular route might feel inclined to see that part of the coast from a greater height. Thirdly, it will attract all who enjoy an exhilarating walk over high downs and a minimal contact with other people while, at the same time, being always within easy reach of bus-stops and railway stations. This makes it a useful walk for those with limited time and return journeys to think of.

At one time or another I had walked along sections of this high-level route, sometimes without realizing that I was on an alternative to the Dorset Coast Path and often before the Coast Path itself was opened in 1974. As it is an official alternative, I knew when I began this book that I must walk over and describe the whole length of it, but I looked on it rather as a duty walk. I found how wrong I was when I enjoyed every part of it immensely and went over several parts of it again. I am sure that many of us are instinctively dismissive about this alternative because we think of it as a *Coast* Path. But this is not a compulsory inland routing like those on other sections of the South West Way, which exercise the persuasive energies of the Association in efforts to remove obstacles from the path. No walker *has* to take the alternative but those who do will, I believe, find it as pleasant going as I have done.

1 West Bexington to the Hardy Monument

Instead of carrying along the path to the inside of the Chesil Beach after West Bexington car-park (*see* p.135, 4: West Bay to Abbotsbury), turn left into the road that goes up the hill and inland, past the café on the left and the Manor House Hotel (which has a bar) on the right, past the Manor House Farm which, in season, displays for sale on top of the garden-wall fruit and vegetables unsprayed and untainted by the hand of man the chemist. Take what you fancy and put the money into a box: should the farmer or his wife and family be there, replenishing the stocks, they will be delighted to explain points of local topography and to comment on the state of the footpaths.

Ignore the sharp turn to the left that the road makes just past the farm, and go straight up the track to the right of some bungalows, a telephone kiosk, and the Post Office Stores. To westward of the stony track are cultivated fields, and to the right or eastward side are hawthorn, blackthorn, bramble thickets, privet, and honeysuckle draped over all. Further up there is a stone wall on the right with a gateway leading into a clearing among the bushes. To the left is a profusion of deadly nightshade, crowsfoot, and restharrow. At a fork in the track take the right-hand path, which is less rocky than the track leading from the road. It rises gradually between blackthorn, gorse, elder, and hawthorn. Soon there is what seems almost like an old paved road, the stones set there being so firm and regular, and the track opens out near the top to a spreading view of the Chesil Beach, and down over the Manor House Farm, the hotel and the bungalows and car-park of West Bexington. The track comes out on the crest of Limekiln Hill on the Bridport-Abbotsbury A3157 road, at a point that gives a panorama, on a clear day, of the distance travelled, sometimes as far west as Start Point.

Looking back slightly to landward and west, there is a knoll wooded with deciduous and coniferous trees. This is Knoll Plantation and on top of the knoll is a much-vandalized Coast

Guard lookout that dates back to the time of the threatened French invasion under Bonaparte. The knoll is in the parish of Puncknowle, which on some maps is spelled Punknoll – so to say Puncknowle Knoll is something of a tautology.

A hundred yards east along the road a wooden gate on the right leads into rough pasture, with patches of bramble but not much sign of a path. Although there is still a vestige of a stony track here and there, do not be misled into taking it, because it leads nearer and nearer to the sea and eventually to Labour in Vain farm, now in the keeping of the National Trust. In fact the Coast Path should take the walker around the lower flank of Tulk's Hill and up to the road again. The route is immensely difficult to follow in any season but particularly so in late spring and summer. Perhaps in winter it is possible to pick one's way through the thicket but it is always better, to my mind, to skirt along the top edge of this bushy area. At one point on the right there is a stone ruin with a low chasm on the seaward side, and out of an archway in the ruin runs a rudimentary stream. Perhaps I cheated a bit by following hoofmarks and horse-droppings until I crossed a stone wall and then came out again on the Bridport-Abbotsbury road. It is impossible to get lost if that road is kept in sight, and a course, chiefly parallel but gradually converging towards it, is followed.

Cross the main road to a gate on the other side, which leads into a pasture rising to the Iron-Age earthworks of Abbotsbury Castle. There is a path below the crest of the Castle running between it and the road, but this is much more boring than climbing to the top of the earthworks. Beyond a triangulation pillar there is a small plateau, which ends with a stile over a fence and a steep but short descent to a gravel pit on a narrow metalled private road, leading past a wood to Ashley Chase Farm. Cross this road to a stile and take the broad path across Wear's Hill, a walk that induces a fine sense of smug superiority when looking down on to the motor-cars rushing along the road below. A pair of buzzards wheeled and planed above me, their feathers gleaming grey-fawn in the thundery sunshine.

On top of Wear's Hill are small and abrupt tumuli and a small

ruined lookout from the Second World War. Over towards the
sea lie the massed green of the ilexes and sub-tropical trees of
Abbotsbury Gardens. Keep to the right of a kind of giant
boxing-ring, surrounded by barbed-wire and enclosing a concrete
building overgrown with nettles and brambles and surmounted
by a rusty white metal triangle – which I suppose is a sea mark of
some kind. Keep to the highest contour of this ridge, over Wears
Hill and White Hill, which is the old Dorset Coastal Ridgeway,
and ignore the path going inland and down to some woods. Soon
the Hardy Monument comes into view on the crest of Black
Down. The path is not easy to follow when the grass is high but
keep the Monument in sight. Leave the Dutch barn on the left
and walk on and out to a metalled road, Bishop's Road. This
climbs from Abbotsbury and has on the left on the way up a
well-restored limekiln and a pleasantly set-out little car-park with
tables and benches for those who want to picnic, or sit and take in
the Chesil Bank's scimitar curve towards the rocky mass of
Portland. A farmer feeding his calves in a field beside Bishop's
Road said, 'What a wonderful old coastline we have here. Could
do with a little more sand along it, couldn't it?' 'Yes,' I replied,
'and with a lot less threat of more nuclear power-stations along
here.' 'Ah, they'll change it more than the tides have in a
thousand years – and drive away more people too.'

A hundred yards along Bishop's Road a Coast Path sign points
right to a path that follows the ridge in a predictable way, passing
a stone circle, and coming out alongside some farm buildings, a
milking-shed and a fine old stone barn. From there a short farm
road leads to a cattle-grid and a gateway out on to the crest of
Portesham Hill and the road leading down to the village of
Portesham. Turn left along this road for a hundred yards, to a
Coast Path Inland Route sign to the right. This leads over a stile
and through a hedge and then over another single stile into a
pasture. Do not cross the pasture in a direct line, but look out for
the path veering slightly to the right: it leads, in a few hundred
yards, to the restored burial-chamber known as the Hell Stone.

The Hell Stone is the incorrectly rebuilt chamber of a Neolithic
long barrow, consisting of nine upright stones and a capstone. It

has nothing to do with Hades but might have a lot to do with *Halig* – holy; or with Hel, the goddess of the dead. It dates from about 4000 BC, and a well-meaning but misguided attempt to restore it in 1866 put it together wrongly.

The Path turns at almost right-angles northwards, by way of Black Down Barn and some somewhat battered farm buildings with veteran and vintage farm machinery dotted around them. Take the path forking up to the left through a plantation of fir and beech spattered with foxglove and honeysuckle, and when clear of the trees look back now and then to the stupendous views of the Chesil and Portland, and westward to Golden Cap and the curve of Lyme Bay. Coming out on to the top of Black Down the terrain seems to be a mixture of mountain, moor and heath, with bright white scree held together by the heather, and here and there tall bracken and a few scrubby conifers.

Visible from many distant points of Dorset, the Hardy Monument, which now comes into sight beyond what look like abandoned gravel pits, is not as large as one might think. It is 70ft high and was built in 1844 to the design of Arthur Dyke Acland-Troyte as a monument to Admiral Sir Thomas Masterman Hardy (1769–1839), Nelson's flag-captain on *Victory* and in whose arms Nelson died when he received his fatal wound. Hardy was made First Sea Lord in 1830 and became a vice-admiral in 1837. He was born at Kingston Russell House, less than three miles to the north-east of 'Blackon', and he lived both as a boy and again late in life in Portesham, his beloved 'Possum'. The Monument is thought by many visitors to Dorset to have been erected to Thomas Hardy the writer, and it has attracted some uncomplimentary descriptions – such as its resemblance to a factory chimney with a crinoline, a chess pawn, or an old-fashioned 'daffodil telephone receiver set on end'. But it is an excellent seamark that would have pleased Thomas Masterman Hardy, and it merits its National Trust guardianship.

2 Hardy Monument to Bincombe

Come out on to the main road by the Monument and turn right: a hundred yards downhill is a signpost marking a bridleway right 'to Corton Hill 2 miles'. This is a clear track, broad enough to be scored by the tyres of farmers' Land Rovers; it must have been marked by human feet, by sheep, cattle, and horses, for many centuries, for it is part of the old Dorset Coastal Ridgeway. At first the track rises gradually between gorsy banks and then, beyond a farm gate, comes out to pasture on the left. On the right, below in the folded green and deserted hollows of the downs, there is a ruin of almost ecclesiastical appearance, partnered in its grey solitude, when I last saw it, by an elder tree in flower surrounded by black and white heifers.

Keep straight along this track, which here and there is surfaced by mostly unbroken flints. Looking back, the Hardy Monument above its triangular wood of conifers looks very impressive. At one point there is every reason for thinking that, as the Path begins to go downhill, one should have taken a branch to the left; but, Harry Lauder-like, keep right on to the end of the road – and what a road it is, between gorse and bramble, foxglove and cow parsley, with nothing in the valleys to the right but a ruined farm-house and with every step sight of Portland clearer and more extraordinary. Now and then a segment of the Fleet is visible between the hills. On the better pasture are heifers and young bullocks, but on the higher and poorer ground are many sheep, snow-white if the rain has been particularly heavy and possessed of that alertness of upland sheep, so different from those poor animals who drag around in their woollen overcoats weighed down with lowland mud. The sheep look up from cropping grass on the crests of Bronze Age round barrows, some with brown or black faces, only horns needed to make them into convincing downland chamois.

It is as well that it is nearly impossible to go wrong on this Path because there is little waymarking, not a dash of yellow paint anywhere – yet at one point, beside a dilapidated iron farm gate, there is what looks like a signpost that has lost its arms. The gates along this stretch are on rickety hinges with orange twine holding them closed, the top bars garnished with barbed wire but leaving just enough bare at one end for a walker to climb over. If walking at dusk or at night, look carefully before grasping a gate.

The feeling on this Ridgeway, of a most ancient road used since men first inhabited these islands, is very strong. Drystone walls look as if they have been raised on older stone walls that have subsided into the ground, and often on the southern side of the path over Bronkham Hill there is a wall made of upended slabs of stone in the way that North Wales farmers near slate quarries make slate fences. Some of these stones are so rectangular that one expects to find them engraved with the names of dead drovers.

The track veers slightly to the left and drops gently to an angled crossroads, where the road going north-east runs between Great Hill and Ridge Bottom with tumuli dotted beside it, until it passes through Grove Hill Bottom and emerges in the village of Martinstown, or Winterbourne St Martin. Running south-west, the track crosses Corton Down and joins the metalled road just to the north of Corton Hill. But our Path goes due east and straight, flanked by barrows, the furzy pastures now having given way to undulating fields of barley and wheat, or plough, according to the season. The drystone wall to the right of the Path shows the way ahead, rising gradually over Ridge Hill, while to the right is that unfamiliar view of Portland seen across Weymouth in which the church spires thrust up above the roofs, and where at Portland the buildings cling to the seemingly precipitous northern face of what from here seems very much a true island.

There are still occasional gates across the track, and at the side of one of them, in a landscape still studded with barrows, is a large stone marking the boundary of the Borough of Weymouth and Melcombe Regis. The track along Ridge Hill passes 38 barrows on the seaward side, presumably all the responsibility of the Weymouth Borough Council. The last gate across the track is just beyond a triangulation pillar, and on the right of the track there is a radio mast surrounded by a barbed-wire fence. When I was there, piles of building material and wheelbarrows indicated that something was going to be built there – nothing too large, I hope. The mast itself is a very fragile looking one, pinned to its spot by thread-thin wires. Looking back from here to the Monument (standing on what now seems like a well-wooded hill) and taking another quick look at the radio mast, one finds them both puny in comparison with the ramparts of Maiden Castle beyond the valley of the South Winterbourne (there is a North Winterborne stream and another group of Winterborne villages in central and east Dorset). This is one of the most satisfactory places from which to appreciate the size and grandeur of one of the largest earthworks in Britain: a causewayed camp of c.3500 BC, above which lies an Iron Age fort begun c.350 BC and enlarged during the next 400 years. A footpath to Maiden Castle leaves the Ridgeway half-way between the Corton Down-Great Hill crossroads and the Weymouth boundary-stone.

Beyond the radio mast the track broadens, with cultivated fields on the left and a hawthorn hedge on the right, beyond a good show of poppies in a slender cultivated strip. The track drops gently to a very wide and strong metal farm gate that looks as if it might be expecting tanks, and opens on to the B3159 road from Martinstown through Gould's Bottom to Upwey with its much-publicized wishing-well where King George III drank the waters (*see* p.148, 7: Weymouth) from what was to become the Ascot Gold Cup. Upwey has an attractive village street with an elegant manor-house (1639), seventeenth-eighteenth century Westbrook House, and Upwey Mill, built in 1802, with the corrugated-iron roof to the hoist added a good bit later.

Across the B3159 from the gateway is another boundary-stone and a large road sign proclaiming 'Weymouth'. Take the broad track to the left of these boundary signs, through the right-hand gate. The track has cultivated fields to the right, and on the left drystone walls and barbed-wire, with pasture beyond. At the top of this slight rise there is a wide view over to the left of Dorchester and Maiden Castle, beyond a scrubby triangle of firs, small beech and horse-chestnut trees. Take the left-hand of two gates here, and carry on straight ahead, with open fields still on the right, and on the left a fine example of a drystone wall – here and there a hawthorn has got the upper hand and pushed the wall into drunken leanings. The track now descends, and when you are within about fifty yards of the main A354 Dorchester–Weymouth road, there is a crossroads in the track. Turn to the right here and

watch out for a narrow break in the hedge on the left where some
kind soul has considerately tied plastic fertilizer-bags over the top
strand of barbed-wire. This track runs parallel to the main road.
Cross over the narrow field between the track and the road, and
look for a wooden signpost with a yellow arrow pointing to where
you have just come from. The Countryside Commission's
admirable Long Distance Footpath Guide No 8, *Dorset Coast Path*
by Brian Jackman, sends the walker on to the main road for half a
mile instead of taking this parallel track, a public right-of-way.
This is potentially highly dangerous, particularly in summer or at
dusk, for high banks fall sheer to the tarmac and the brow of the
hill limits visibility at a spot where the traffic is as furious and
plentiful as it is fast. Rather than walk along there, I would, again,
prefer to come out on to the road and cross straight over into the
minor road to Broadmayne, along which you walk a little further
until you rejoin the Path, running in from the right. Incidentally,
the Bartholomew 1:100000 Dorset map shows the Alternative
Coast Path on the track which I advocate.

Facing the wooden signpost on the A354 there is a green metal
Bridleway signpost. The track now goes briskly up and down
along the scarp of Bincombe Down. To the right there is the vista
of Weymouth rooftops with Portland beyond, all of it on the far
side of a deep valley and much dead ground. Below, motor-cars
trundle along the main road and miniature trains run along an
invisible track; here, there is furze and heather, brambles, and
much chalk brought to the surface by rabbits in the many
warrens. Keep straight along, with the barbed-wire fence on the
left, and further over yet the high green fence around some kind
of water-pumping installation just beyond farm buildings, and
two tumuli – all on the left. Head for the black iron gate at the
end of the field; this opens on to the minor road running from
the A354 to Broadmayne. Turn right along this road, where the
verges produce exceptionally fine mallow and toadflax in a
mauve and yellow summer dapple.

On the other side of the stone wall to the left of the road is
Came Down Golf Course, to which in the early years of the
Second World War the Bomb Disposal Section to which I

belonged used to bring the unexploded German bombs that we had dug up all over Dorset. Life there is more hazardous now: a large red-lettered notice warns of 'Danger from driven golf-balls' – another instance of dangerous driving.

At a signpost topped by 'Came Wood' there is a right-angle turn left to Dorchester (3½ miles). Immediately opposite this turning is a farm gate hung with two red triangles, presumably to warn yet other dangerous drivers. Beside it a wooden signpost has a red circle on it and is marked 'Bincombe ½ mile'.

A broad track goes down between cultivated fields to a farm gate opening on to a bend in a metalled private road leading up to Hill Barn. Turn right, down to a large modern barn and a stone house just beyond it. On the right of this private road is a metal sign giving the name of the property as 'Granary'; turn left into

Going down to Bincombe village

the public road that goes fairly steeply between high banks down
to Bincombe, a hamlet of stone cottages and farm buildings
seemingly little changed – except that it now has half the
population it had a century ago.

3 **Bincombe to Osmington Mills**

The right-hand side of this village street is occupied by farm
buildings, and the cottages on the left stand on a stone terrace
that forms a footpath which in places is some three feet above the
surface of the road. Opposite a farmyard is Dairy House, which
has two corbels supported by figures, one of a man standing and
the other of a seated woman. They have been reset on either side
of the central upper window. Newman and Pevsner in their *Dorset*
volume of the 'Buildings of England' series (Penguin) describe
them as being 'originally of quite good quality, perhaps mid-14th
century. What did they come from? A monument or shrine, one
would say, rather than a full-scale building.' In order to
photograph them I stood on a cattle trough in the farmyard, and,
hearing a plop in the water below, I thought I had dropped the
lens cap. But when I looked down I saw two large goldfish
swishing around in the muddy water.

The road bends to the right at the foot of the hill, but pay no
attention to this and carry on straight ahead between more farm
buildings towards a tree-shaded lane. Holy Trinity Church, on
the right, has retained some early thirteenth-century features, but
suffered the usual Victorian restoration. One is not sure how
much was taken away, but mercifully not much was added. It is
one of the few churches I know to have a stone altar rail in the
form of a 3-ft high colonnade. The churchyard has plots of bright
flowers, and one can look over the wall into the farmyard below.
Somewhere in the churchyard, now lost, are the graves of two
22-year-old German soldiers who deserted from the Duke of
York's Hussars (the 'grand old Duke of York' who marched his
men up hill and then down), landed in Jersey thinking that it was
France, and were brought back to be shot on 30 June 1801. The
burial entry is in the Bincombe Parish Register, and Hardy based
a story on the incident – 'The Melancholy Hussar of the German
Legion'.

Beyond the church, the track forks where an ash tree stands on a triangular green. Take the left fork up a stony track under the lee of Bincombe Hill, which is scored by corrugations – more likely made by sheep than by man – and outcrops of rock. This hill is blessed with a wide variety of the small flowers of the chalk, mostly blue or mauve – such as eyebright, wild thyme, felwort, creeping toadflax and ivy-leaved toadflax.

The top of Bincombe Hill is no longer the encampment of the German Legion but is crowned by an enormous pylon whose regiment marches across the downs in both directions. Chalbury Hill-Fort, which encloses over eight acres, is visible over on the right, and the village of Sutton Poyntz is down below.

Go down the slope to a farm gate at the bottom, and out on to a metalled road (narrow, with passing places) that skirts around the base of Chalbury Hill and runs through Coombe Valley. Turn left and walk along this road for a few hundred yards to just

Spring Bottom, Preston

beyond Green Hill Barton on the right. Here the road forks at
Coombe Valley signpost, left to Whitcombe and Dorchester, and
right to Sutton Poyntz and Preston. Take the right fork, and at
the top of a slight rise, where Portland comes into sight once
more, take the farm gate to the left. Continue up a track to
another Weymouth and Melcombe Regis boundary-stone on
West Hill. Looking back, there is a group of six barrows on the
skyline known as Bincombe Bumps.

The track goes straight along the top of West Hill with a line of
eleven tumuli to the left of the path, while on the right there is a
drop to a deep green bowl from which comes the sound of
running water. This oasis-like spot is called Spring Bottom. There
is a meeting-place of five footpaths at the ruins of Northdown
Barn, and beyond the ruins a signpost gives 1½ miles back to
Bincombe, Abbotsbury 9 miles, and to the right Osmington 1½
miles. Follow this right turn along a broad green road for about a
hundred yards, to the next fork. Take the right-hand track,
through a gate into a flinty field with a triangulation pillar in it
and a round barrow on the right. The cut hay was being turned
by tractor in this field when I went through it, but nothing had
been cut on another barrow in a corner of the field which had a
magnificent show of bladder campion, knapweed, corn spurrey,
sow-thistle, dandelion, clover, kidney vetch and bird's-foot trefoil.
There were many many more flowers, some lingering lustily on
from the spring, others exuberantly declaring high summer, and,
I have to confess, all too many of which I could not recall the
names. That barrow at the edge of the hayfield was one of the
most delightful flower-beds I have ever seen, and I picked my
way up the side as carefully as in a garden to look over Weymouth
and Portland Harbour from the top.

Follow the path along the left of this field to a gate at the end,
where East Hill gives way to White Horse Hill and a wooden
signpost gives 2 miles to Bincombe, 10 miles to Abbotsbury, 2
miles straight ahead to Poxwell (diplomatically pronounced
Pokeswell) and, the right-hand fork, 1 mile Osmington and 8
miles to Lulworth. This is the one we take. Fifty yards further on
there is another signpost which I went to look at out of curiosity:

The track from the top of White Horse Hill, down to Osmington village

King George III on his way from Weymouth, cut into White Horse Hill

it points repetitively to Poxwell and Lulworth but gives a footpath to the left leading to Broadmayne (no distance given, but it must be about 2 miles).

The path down to Osmington leaves the crest of White Horse Hill just to the east of the 1815 figure of George III on horseback riding away from Weymouth. At the foot of the track, on the outskirts of Osmington, look back at him, albeit at a slight angle, to get an idea of how, unwittingly, you have been strolling along the top of a picture-frame.

The track turns into a metalled road with houses on the left, most of them concealed behind hedges, and then climbs slightly, overhung by trees, until it passes Charity Farm and Osmington Forge and Horticultural Engineers on the left. Charity Farm is a long stone house built with the house and cow-byre in a single range. Unfortunately the roof is of corrugated-iron, perhaps as advertising for the forge. Further up the road the thatched post office stands on a corner; most of the houses are thatched and have colourful gardens. One could easily pass the church which is nearly hidden on the right among trees. In fact, the whole of Osmington village is cupped in a little dell: had it been closer to the sea, it might have been taken up by the Regency sea-bathing society. The White House, built about 1830 and boldly bow-windowed, echoes the Charmouth, Lyme Regis, and Weymouth of the period.

St Osmund's Church dates mainly from 1846, and has a memorial to a member of the Warham family, one of whom was Archbishop of Canterbury in the early sixteenth century. There are three crudely lettered inscriptions. One is in Latin: 'I have come into harbour. Farewell Hope and farewell Fortune. I am done with you. Sport now with others' – a sentiment worthy of Thomas Hardy. The second states: 'Man's Life. Man is a glas: Life is as water that's weakly walled about: Sinne brings in Death: Death breakes the glas: So runnes the water out. Finis.' And the third is not exactly borne on wings of joy either: 'Here is not the man who in his life with every man had law and strife.'

John Constable stayed in the vicarage here during his honeymoon in 1816 when he painted 'Osmington Village' and

The forge at Osmington

'Weymouth Bay'. Opposite the church is Rosemary Cottage, which has a Dorset crafts shop and where Ann Clark serves delicious cream-teas indoors, or in the enclosed garden when it is fine.

Carry on up to the main road, the A353 from Weymouth to Warmwell Cross; turn left past the Sunray pub and the lovely seventeenth-century buildings of East Farm, and watch out for a newish concrete driveway to a house on the right of the road. If a very sharp eye is used, a footpath sign will be seen, much discoloured by weather and seeming to try to hide against an ivy-covered dead elm, as it whispers, 'Footpath to Osmington Mills'. (The concrete drive to the house curves to the right but on the other side of it is a farm gate with a yellow arrow on it.) This footpath, not easy to follow, runs over the brow of the hill and the fields, crossing hedges by stiles and keeping parallel to the road to Osmington Mills, which it eventually joins (through a tree-overhung and water-rutted path) to come out opposite a tall old pine standing in the grounds of the Osmington Holiday Club. Beyond the pine can be glimpsed the club's swimming-pool. Turn right down the road, on the left of which is a deep cleft with tree-covered banks. There are caravans at the bottom of this narrow valley, the Streamside Caravan Park. The road ends at the Smugglers' Inn where the Coast Path is rejoined.

Walking on the Chesil Beach

Introduction

The Chesil Beach (from Saxon *cisel* – shingle) is a bank of pebbles that runs from the 'Isle' of Portland for ten miles to join the Dorset mainland at the west end of Abbotsbury Swannery which, with the Fleet (a narrow sea loch or lagoon), separates the Chesil from the coast. The Beach continues westwards from Abbotsbury for seven miles as part of the main shore to West Bay, broken only by Burton Mere which may be all that remains of a longer stretch of water. I described in *Dorset Villages* this '. . . natural formation, unique in Europe, a Dorset barrier-reef with a reputation for mackerel, shipwreck, dangerous currents and a variety of cast-ashore objects, from ships' boilers to silver ingots, exotic plants from the Americas and, in 1757, a mermaid – "no beauty" commented those who saw her.'

Daniel Defoe, in *A Tour through the Whole Island of Great Britain* (1724–6), wrote of '(The Isle of Portland) . . . hence it is that our best and whitest free stone comes, with which the cathedral of St Paul's, the Monument, and all the publick edifices of London, are chiefly built . . . Tho' Portland stands a league off the main land of Britain, yet it is almost joyn'd by a prodigious riffe of beach, that is to say, of small stones cast up by the sea, which runs from the island so near the shore of England, that they ferry over with a boat and a rope, the water not being above half a stone's throw over; and the said riffe of beach ending, as it were, at that inlet of water, turns away west, and runs parallel with the shore quite to Abbotsbury . . . On the inside of this beach, and between it and the land, there is an inlet . . . this inlet opens at about two miles west, and grows very broad, and makes a kind of lake within the land of a mile and a half broad, and near three miles in length, the breadth unequal. At the farthest edge west of this water is a large duck-coy, and the verge of the water well grown with wood, and proper groves of trees of cover for the foul; in the open lake, or broad part, is a continual assembly of swans . . . Here they are protected, and here they breed in abundance . . .'

Nothing much has changed along the Chesil Beach in the past 250 years, but a lot has happened there. A century after Defoe wrote, there was the 'Outrage' when the sea breached the 'reef of

beach' and destroyed most of the village and the church of East
Fleet; and in 1839 the October gales hoisted *Ebenezer* on to the top
of the Chesil (*see* p.143, 6: Abbotsbury to Weymouth). In
November 1795 a thousand people were drowned from a West
Indies-bound fleet, and in the same month 215 soldiers and 9
women of *Golden Grove* perished opposite Langton Fleet; 300
drowned when *Abergavenny* sank in February 1805; and in March
1815 the East Indiaman *Alexander* foundered with the loss of 140
souls. Sometimes human violence was added to that of the sea. In
1748 , returning from South America, *Hope* of Amsterdam broke
on the reef. On board was £50,000 in gold, and a treasure-
questing mob held the beach against the authorities for ten days.
When, in 1762, a French man-o'-war foundered, 72 of the crew
got ashore but were robbed and stripped of their clothes by a local
rabble. Instead of holding the sailors as prisoners-of-war, George
III had them clad and sent back to France.

   Strange, inhospitable, noisy and sometimes deafening with the
constant movement of millions of pebbles, the Chesil Beach
provides a walk unlike any other I have ever undertaken. It is a
hard slog, and once on it there is no getting off until Small Mouth
and the Weymouth-Portland road are reached. Nowhere is it
suggested as an alternative to the Coast Path or even to the
Alternative High-Level Path, but it is a challenge to those who
have walked the official routes and feel like changing to
something completely different. I walked it once, at the tail-end
of a February gale, and I have never regretted it.

The Chesil Beach: Abbotsbury to Ferry Bridge (Weymouth)
At the point where the road comes down past Abbotsbury
Sub-Tropical Gardens (*see* p.137, 5: Abbotsbury) go straight ahead
along the broad rough track on the landward side of the Chesil
Beach, behind which the sea is hidden. Where some marshy scrub
marks the end of the unofficial car-park, take the path to the
right of the reedy swamp which is really the forerunner of the
Swannery and the Fleet. Beyond the reeds and inland, St
Catherine's Chapel stands on top of its hill. To the other side, on

Looking westwards along the Chesil Beach from above Fortuneswell, Portland

top of the 30ft-high bank of pebbles, is a ruined wartime pillbox, and further along are the 'dragons' teeth', now carious with age, planted across the beach from the waterline to the edge of the Swannery, which were intended to halt the invading German tanks. The thick beds of whispering reeds, a whisper of small dry bones rather than of sibilant confidences, thin out into the wide water of the Swannery, some 600 years old and now a nature reserve.

To keep as far from it as possible, so as not to cause alarm among the occupants, I climbed to the top of the Chesil and plodded along on the shingle which here is roughly the size of hazelnuts. It has often been said that local fishermen landing on the Chesil in the dark can tell where they are by the size of the stones, which are small as gravel at West Bay and increase to the girth of goose-eggs and footballs close to Portland. I could look down on the Swannery at the black speckle of coot and tern and the white splashes of mute swans. On the seaward side, waves as high as Abbotsbury Barn were bringing in great balks of timber from a ship lately gone down off Guernsey, tossing them like cabers on to the steep-shelving, growling shingle.

It is a hard trudge along the top and when I came level with the end of the nature reserve I found some welcome variety by walking on the Fleet shore where a tangle of dead weed lies as thick as coco-matting. There is an occasional tarred wooden shack for the storing of nets and other fishing-gear, and a few boats drawn up and over to the landward side. In a sudden squall of rain and hail I sheltered under the friendly upturned *Kate*, and ate my hard-boiled eggs and cheese.

Apart from the waterfowl on the Swannery, I saw few birds during my walk because of the still-roaring sou'-wester. Near the edge of the Fleet, hares started up from their forms in Dorset heath and ling to rattle and zigzag over the slanting shingle. They were big and well-covered, but there seems little for them to eat and the water of the Fleet is brackish from the seepage through the shingle. Hares can swim, so maybe they cross to pastures on the other side at narrows like Langton Hive Point or Herbury. An old Dorset farmer on the mainland claimed to have seen hares swimming in the Fleet and he believed that the Beach colony of *Lepus timidus* commuted to the mainland vegetable gardens on calm summer nights.

But it was no calm summer night when I was walking there, and when I was on top of the ridge again some particularly high waves came crashing in and the thought of the 'Outrage' crossed my mind. If history were to be repeated, I should at least be washed into the Fleet and possibly on to the land beyond. When I came across the remains of an aeroplane engine, the block scored by pebbles, and the edges and corners rounded away, I wondered if the crew had survived and how they got off the Beach. Were they British or were they German, and if the latter, what did they make of the strange reef on which they were landed and stranded? Perhaps like the German Legion Hussars from

Bincombe, they thought they were safely in France?

Victor Hugo was a refugee from France when he likened Portland to a bird's head and neck lying on the sea. I could see what he meant, as the 'Isle' is in sight throughout the whole walk. There is not much on the landward side of the Fleet but fields and trees, as reminders that green things do grow close to the bare reef. Closer to Weymouth, with Portland now dotted with houses that seem to stand on one another's eaves, the mainland takes on a somewhat military air, with Chickerell Camp, the rifle-range, and, where the Fleet is squeezed to its narrowest point, the military installation around which the Coast Path has to make a detour (*see* p.143, 7: Weymouth). The buildings of Wyke Regis seem to crowd towards the Fleet, and one wonders what on earth one is doing plodding along out there, so near and yet so far, on top of a pebble reef where water seems about to close in on all sides.

The Chesil Beach carries on as an isthmus to Portland where it ends at the village of Chesil, but I walked only far enough to find a way of getting up and on to the Weymouth-Portland road. A turn to the left, and a couple of hundred yards up, the road reaches the Ferry Bridge, under which the Fleet joins up with Portland Harbour at Small Mouth. There are buses to Weymouth and Portland, and the Coast Path actually crosses the road by the Ferry Bridge pub, formerly the Royal Victoria, (*see* p.144, 7: Weymouth), so walkers can go 'legit' again.

Appendix
Useful Information and Addresses

Backpackers' Club	Eric Gurney, 20 St Michael's Road, Tilehurst, Reading, Berkshire
Buses	Bere Regis and District Motor Service, 7 Bridport Road, Dorchester (tel: Dorchester 2992)
	Dorset Queen Coaches, East Chaldon, Dorchester (tel: Warmwell 0305)
	Hants and Dorset Bus Co., The Square, Bournemouth (tel: Bournemouth 23371)
	National Travel (South West) Ltd, Coach Station, Cheltenham, Glos (tel: Cheltenham 519926)
	G.E. Nightingale, Barn Lane Cottage, Budleigh Salterton, Devon (tel: Budleigh Salterton 2700)
	Plymouth City Transport, Milehouse, Plymouth, Devon (tel: Plymouth 68000)
	South Dorset Coaches, East Street, Corfe Castle, Wareham, Dorset (tel: Corfe Castle 444)
	Tally Ho! Coaches Ltd, Industrial Estate, Kingsbridge, Devon (tel: Kingsbridge 3230)
	Western National Omnibus Co Ltd, Head Office, National House, Queen Street, Exeter (tel: Exeter 74191)
Camping	Leaflets and information about camp-sites may be obtained from: Devon County Tourist Officer, County Hall, Topsham, Devon

Camping   County Public Relations and Information
                          Officer, County Hall, Dorchester, Dorset.
                          The Camping Club of Great Britain and
                          Ireland Ltd, 11 Lower Grosvenor Place,
                          London, SW1. A Site Guide is available to
                          members.

Commons,   25a, Bell Street, Henley-on-Thames,
Open Spaces   Oxfordshire.
and Footpaths
Preservation
Society

Council for the   4 Hobart Place, London SW1.
Protection of
Rural England

Countryside   John Dower House, Crescent Place,
Commission   Cheltenham, Glos. Information available about
                          all the Long Distance Paths.

Ferries   Walkers along the South Devon and Dorset
                          section of the South West Way have to cross a
                          number of rivers. Some, like those on the
                          Dorset coast, are crossed easily by bridges or do
                          not form real estuaries because they sink into
                          the shingle before reaching the shore. There is
                          only one Dorset ferry on the Path and that is an
                          optional one across Weymouth Harbour, to
                          which the alternative is a pleasant
                          twenty-minute walk along the quays and round
                          by Town Bridge to the other side. Along the
                          South Devon Coast Path there are seven rivers
                          to cross: one of them has no ferry at all, and
                          some of the others have a somewhat chancy
                          service. The following is basic information, but
                          details of Tide Tables for the whole Peninsula

Ferries

Path are printed in the annual *South West Way: a Complete Guide to the Coastal Path*.

River Yealm

There is a triangular crossing between Warren Point, Newton Ferrers and Noss Mayo. The ferry is stationed below the Yealm Hotel. From the other two points, shout or wave to attract attention, or telephone in advance to:
Len Carter and Son,
Riverslea,
Yealm Road,
Newton Ferrers. (Tel: Plymouth 872210)
May-September, 7 days a week, 0900–1700, but May-mid July 0900–1800, as required.

River Erme

This is the river that has no ferry. The Erme can often be waded from Mothecombe to Wonwell, one hour each side of low water, at the old ford, as described on p.40. In times of heavy seas, or flood-water coming down the Yealm, make the detour to Sequers Bridge up-river on the A379.

River Avon

The ferry is seasonal and is operated from the Bantham side by:
H. Cater,
Yorick,
West Buckland,
Kingsbridge. (Tel: Thurlestone 593)
Two weeks at Easter, and from May-end September, Monday-Saturday 1000–1100 and 1500–1600, Sundays in July and August only. Shout across the river for the ferry.
    It is possible to wade the Avon at low tide,

Ferries crossing from the pine trees in the hedge on the Bigbury or Cockleridge side and heading for the castellated building on the far shore. But it is more dangerous than the Erme, and has deep channels and soft sand in places. Above all, do not attempt to wade across at what looks like the narrowest and most suitable point because the channel is deep there and there are strong currents (see p.44)

Salcombe Harbour
The crossing is from Salcombe quay to East Portlemouth and is operated by:
The Salcombe Ferry Co Ltd,
8 Currer Street,
Bradford,
West Yorkshire. (Tel: Bradford 28375, or the Salcombe boat-house Salcombe 2061) Seven days a week throughout the year. Summer 0700–2050, Sundays 0800–1950: Winter 0700–1950, Sundays 0800–1850.

River Dart
The Lower Ferry takes both cars and pedestrians over to Kingswear and is operated by:
The South Hams District Council,
Ferry Manager's Department,
The Square,
Kingswear,
Dartmouth. (Tel: Kingswear 342)
Seven days a week throughout the year, 0700–2255, Sundays 0800–2255. Six-minute service in summer, 12-minute service in winter. Last ferry from Dartmouth at 2245, and from Kingswear 2255. The Lower Ferry foot passenger service is operated by:

Ferries   Dart Pleasure Craft Ltd,
                       5 Lower Street,
                       Dartmouth. (Tel: Dartmouth 3144)
                       April-October, Monday to Saturday 0700–2300
                       October-April, Monday to Saturday 0730–1830

                       River Teign
                       The crossing is between Shaldon Beach and
                       Teignmouth Harbour Beach and is operated
                       by:
                       Teignbridge District Council,
                       Channel View,
                       Teignmouth. (Tel: Teignmouth 6271)
                       October-March, Monday to Friday 0800–1700
                       March-October, every day 0800–1700 and up
                       to 2200 in the summer. When the ferry is not in
                       operation walk to Shaldon Bridge, less than
                       half a mile inland, and cross there.

                       River Exe
                       Between Starcross and Exmouth a ferry is
                       operated by:
                       The Devon Dock, Pier and Steamship Co Ltd,
                       Dock Office,
                       Exmouth. (Tel: Exmouth 72009)
                       Between the beginning of May and the end of
                       September, eight sailings on weekdays,
                       Saturdays 6 sailings, Sundays 5 sailings. The
                       alternatives are to catch a bus from Cockwood
                       or Starcross to Exeter, 20 miles inland, and
                       thence a bus to Exmouth; or take a train from
                       Dawlish Warren and change at Exeter for
                       Exmouth.

Long Distance   The Secretary,
Walkers'   11 Thorn Bank, Onslow Village,
Association   Guildford, Surrey

Lulworth Range Walks

The Dorset Coast Path through the Lulworth Ranges are open most weekends throughout the year, for about three weeks at Christmas, a week at Easter, a week at the beginning of June and all the time from the end of July to mid-September. It is always advisable to check with the Range Officer (tel: Bindon Abbey 462721 ext. 859, 0800–1700)

National Trust

Enquiries to National Trust Membership Department, PO Box 30, Beckenham, Kent. National Trust in Wessex (Avon, Dorset, Somerset, Wiltshire), enquiries to Regional Information Officer, The National Trust Wessex Regional Office, Stourton, nr. Warminster, Wiltshire.

The National Trust in Devon, enquiries to Regional Information Officer, Killerton House, Broadclyst, Exeter Devon.

Ordnance Survey Maps

Information and Public Enquiries, Ordnance Survey, Romsey Road, Maybush, Southampton.

Railways

The South Devon and Dorset Coast Paths may be reached by British Rail at Plymouth, Torbay, Teignmouth, Dawlish, Exmouth, Weymouth, Poole, Bournemouth. The Path may also be reached at a number of other points by a combination of rail and bus. There is also the privately owned Torbay and Dartmouth Steam Railway that runs from Kingswear to Paignton, with all the former dignity and glory of Great Western travel unimpaired.

Ramblers' Association

1–5 Wandsworth Road, London SW8. The RA publishes annually a *Bed, Breakfast and Bus Guide*.

Royal Society for the Protection of Birds   The Lodge, Sandy, Bedfordshire.

South West Way Association   Membership Secretary: Mrs M. Macleod, 1, Orchard Drive, Kingkerswell, Newton Abbot, Devon. (Tel: (08047) 3061)

Tourist Boards   British Tourist Authority, 64 St James's Street, London SW1.
English Tourist Board, 4 Grosvenor Gardens, London SW1.
Southern Tourist Board, The Old Town Hall, Leigh Road, Eastleigh, Hampshire.
West Country Tourist Board, Trinity Court, 37 Southernhay East, Exeter, Devon.
The English Tourist Board publishes the following:
Where to Stay, 10: West Country: Avon, Cornwall, Devon, Somerset, Western Dorset, Wiltshire and the Isles of Scilly
Where to Stay, 11: South of England: Eastern Dorset, Hampshire and the Isle of Wight.
Farmhouses and Bed and Breakfast in England.

Youth Hostels Association   Membership and enquiries to: YHA National Office, Trevelyan House, 8 St Stephen's Hill, St Albans, Herts.
Youth Hostels on the South Devon and Dorset Coast Paths:
Plymouth: Belmont House, Devonport Road, Stoke, Plymouth, Devon (tel: Plymouth 52189).
Bigbury-on-Sea, Kingsbridge, Devon (tel: Bigbury-on Sea 283).
Salcombe: Overbecks, Sharpitor, Salcombe, Devon (tel: Salcombe 2856)

Youth Hostels Association

Start Bay: The Parish Hall, Strete, Dartmouth, Devon (tel: YHA district office, Plymouth 52753)

Beer: Bovey Combe, Townsend, Beer, Seaton, Devon (tel: Seaton 20296).

Bridport: West Rivers House, West Allington, Bridport, Dorset (tel: Bridport 22655) (About 2 miles off route, but there is a Western National bus service from West Bay.)

Litton Cheney: Litton Cheney, Dorchester, Dorset (tel: Longbredy 340). (About $4\frac{1}{2}$ miles off route, no bus.)

Swanage: Cluny, Cluny Crescent, Swanage (tel: Swanage 2113).

Selected Bibliography

BLATCHFORD, ALAN and BARBARA, *The Long Distance Walker's Handbook: a Guide to Long Distance Routes and Challenge Walks*, Greenway, 1980

BURTON, S.H., *Devon Villages*, Robert Hale, 1973

DUERDEN, FRANK, *The Complete Rambler: a Guide to Every Aspect of Walking in Britain*, Mayflower, 1980

GANT, ROLAND, *Dorset Villages*, Robert Hale, 1980

GREENBANK, ANTHONY, *Walking, Hiking and Backpacking*, Constable, 1978

HAMMOND, REGINALD J.W. (ed.), *The Dorset Coast*, Ward, Lock Red Guide, 1969

– *South Devon*, Ward, Lock Red Guide, 1974

HOSKINS, W.G., *Devon*, Collins, 1954

HUNTER, ROB, *The Outdoor Companion*, Constable, 1979

HYLAND, PAUL, *Purbeck: the Ingrained Island*, Gollancz, 1978

JACKMAN, BRIAN, *Dorset Coast Path: Long-Distance Footpath Guide No 8*, HMSO for the Countryside Commission, 1979

JELLICOE, ANN and MAYNE, ROGER, *Devon: a Shell Guide*, Faber & Faber, 1975

LEGG, RODNEY, *Purbeck Island*, Dorset Publishing Co, 1972

LE MESSURIER, BRIAN, *South Devon Coast Path: Long-Distance Footpath Guide No 9*, HMSO for the Countryside Commission, 1980

MILLAR, T.G., *Long Distance Paths of England and Wales*, David and Charles, 1977

NEWMAN, JOHN and PEVSNER, NIKOLAUS, *The Buildings of England: Dorset*, Penguin, 1972

PEVSNER, NIKOLAUS, *The Buildings of England: South Devon*, Penguin, 1952

PITT RIVERS, MICHAEL, *Dorset: a Shell Guide*, Faber & Faber, 1966

PYATT, EDWARD C., Coastal Paths of the South West, David and Charles, 1971

SEYMOUR, JOHN, *The Companion Guide to the coast of South-West England*, Collins, 1974

SMITH, ANTHONY and SOUTHAM, JILL, *Good Beach Guide*, Penguin, 1973

The South West Way: a Complete Guide to the Coastal Path, South West Way Association, published annually

WARD, KEN, and MASON, JOHN H.N., *The South-West Peninsula Coastal Path*, (in 3 vols: 1, *Minehead to St Ives*; 2, *St Ives to Plymouth*; 3, *Plymouth to Poole*), Charles Letts & Co, 1980

WESTACOTT, H.D., *A Practical Guide to Walking the Devon South Coast Path*, Footpath Publications, 1977

—*A Practical Guide to Walking the Dorset Coast Path*, Footpath Publications, 1977

—*A Walker's Handbook*, Penguin, 1978

WILLY, MARGARET, *The South Hams*, Robert Hale, 1955

Youth Hostels Association (England and Wales) Handbook, published annually by the YHA

Index

Abbotsbury, 136–9, 140, 141, 200, 209, 217
  Castle, 136, 199
  Church, 138–9
  Great Tithe Barn, 138, 139, 220
  Sub-Tropical Gardens, 136, 137, 200, 218
  Swannery, 139, 140, 141, 217, 218, 219, 220
Abraham's Hole, 55
Acland-Troyte, Arthur Dyke, 201
Admiral's Hard, 29
Alfred the Great, 186
All Hallows Church, Ringmore, 42
All Saint's Church, Swanage, 187
Allington, 129
Annie's Cottage, 107
Anning, Mary, 119, 120
Anvil Point, 183
Arish Mell, 169–70
Arundell family of Chideock, 124–5
Ashley Chase Farm, 199
Austen, Jane, 14, 119, 150
Avon River, 42, 43, 44
Axe River/Estuary, 101, 102, 103, 104
Axmouth, 106, 107
Ayrmer Cove, 42

Babbacombe, 75, 76
Backwater, Weymouth, 148
Bacon Hole, 166
Ballard Cliff, 187, 191
Ballard Down, 187
Ballard Point, 185, 187
Ballsaddle Rock, 57
Bankes, Henry, 188

Bantham, 43, 44, 45
Bantham Sands, 45
Barler Rock, 57
Bat's Head, 158, 159
Battisborough Island, 39
Beacon Hill, 39, 41
Beacon Road, 71
Beeching, Wilfred, 189
Beer, 101–1, 102, 103
Beer Head, 100, 106, 123
Beerpan Rocks, 188
Beesands, 60
Belle Vue (National Trust), 183
Berry Head, 72, 73–4
Bigbury Bay, 35
Bigbury-on-Sea, 42, 43
Bincleaves Groyne, 146
Bincleaves House, Weymouth, 146
Bincombe, 206, 207–8, 209
Bincombe Bumps, 209
Bincombe Down, 205
Bincombe Hill, 208
Bindon, Viscount, 167
Bindon Abbey, 165, 167
Bindon Hill, 167
Bindon Range, 164
Bishop's Road, 200
Black Down Barn, 201
Black Head, 88, 152
Black Head Ledges, 152
Blacking, Randoll, 129
Blackpool Farm, 64
Blackpool Sands, 64
Black Stone, 58
Blackstone Rocks, 33
Black Ven, 120, 123
Blacker's Hole, 183
Blake, Admiral Robert, 118

Blind Cow Rock, 159
Blue Waters Holiday Village, 144
Bolberry Down, 15, 48
Bolt Head, 35, 48, 49, 50
Bolt Tail, 47, 48
Bournemouth, 188–9, 192, 193,
    194
Bovisand, 30
Bovisand Fort, 31
Bowleaze Cove, 151
Brandy Bay, 171, 173
Brandy Head, 88
Branscombe, 97–9, 101
Branscombe Mouth, 99
Breakwater Fort, 31
Bride River, 130
Bridge Lane, 141
Bridport, 126, 127, 128, 129
Bridport and West Dorset Golf
    Course, 130
Bridport Arms, West Bay, 129
Bridport Harbour, 127, 128
Brien, Sir Guy de, 63
Brit River, 128, 129
Brixham, 74
Broad Bench, 173
Broad Sands, 74
Broadmayne, 205, 211
Bronkham Hill, 203
Broom Cliff, 121
Brownhill Lane, 33
Brownsea Island, 194
Brunel, Isambard, 79–80
Budleigh Bay, 83
Budleigh Salterton, 82, 84, 85, 87
Bull Rock, 159
Bullerstreet Cove, 142
Bullock Cove, 57
Burgh Island, 42, 43
Burney, Fanny, 169
Burning Cliff (National Trust), 155
Burt, George, 184, 185, 186
Burton Bradstock, 130, 131–2

Burton Cliffs, 126, 130, 131
Burton Mere, 134, 217
Buses, 222
Byron, Anne Isabella, Lady, 80

Cable House, 66
Cain's Folly, 121, 123
Came Down Golf Course, 205–6
Camping, 222–3
Canary Ledges, 120
Cannon Cove, 182
Carter, Philip, 57, 197
Castle Ferry, Dartmouth, 67, 69
Catherine of Aragon, 120–1
Cattewater, 30
Chalbury Hill-Fort, 208
Challaborough, 43
Chapel Hill, 139
Chapman's Pool, 177–8, 180–1
Char River, 121
Charity Farm, 211
Charles I, King, 125
Charles II, King, 120, 129
Charles X, King of France, 169
Charlestown, 143
Charmouth, 120–1, 124
Charnel Cove, 173
Chaucer, Geoffrey, 69
Chesil Beach, 14, 62, 108, 123, 128,
    133–4, 135, 139, 140, 141,
    142–3, 198, 200, 201, 217–21
Chesil village, 221
Chichester, Sir Francis, 30
Chickerell Camp, 221
Chickerell Hive Point, 143
Chideock, 124
Chideock Castle, 124–5
Chiselbury Bay, 88
Chit Rock, 91
Christchurch Harbour, 188
Church Living, Branscombe, 98, 99
Churston Cove, 74
Churston Golf Course, 74

Clairet, Clothilde, 189
Clavell, Sir William, 175
Clavell's Hard, 176
Clavel's Tower, 175–6
Clayhanger Farm, 140
Coal Beach, 88
Coast Guard Station caravan park,
    132–3
Cockleridge Strand, 43
Cockpit Head, 167
Cockwood, 79
Cogden Beach, 133–4
Coleridge, Samuel Taylor, 84
Collings, A.G., 59, 60–1
Colmer's Hill, 126, 127
Colyford, 102
Combe Point, 66
Compass Cottage, 68
Compass Cove, 66, 69
Constable, John, 211–12
Cook, Captain, 30
Coombe Valley, 208, 209
Corfe Castle, 177, 178, 187, 188
Corp, John and Eleynore, 64–5
Corton Down, 203, 204
Corton Hill, 202, 203
Courtenay, Viscount, 50
Courtenay Walk, 50, 51
Cow and Calf rocks, 159
Crab and Crater, 57
Crab Ledge, 88
Creech Hill, 171
Cremyll Ferry, 29, 30
Cuddle, 176
Cynewulf, King of West Saxony,
    117

Dancing Ledge, 182–3
Danger Point, 87, 88
Dart Estuary/River, 43, 68, 69, 70
Dartmoor, 43, 78
Dartmouth, 69–71, 75
Dartmouth Castle, 69–70

Dartmouth Harbour, 64
Dartmouth Naval College, 71
Dawlish, 78–9
Deckler's Cliff, 56
Deer Park Holiday Estate, 65
Defoe, Daniel, 118–19, 217
Devon, Earl of, 50
Devon Bird-watching and
    Preservation Society, 62
Devonport, 29
Devon Trust for Nature
    Conservation, 59
Dixon, Dr Mary, 44
Doghouse Hill, 125
Dorchester, 204, 206, 209
Dorset Coastal Ridgeway, 200, 202
    204
Dowlands Landslip, 104–7
Drake, Sir Francis, 29–30
Drake's or St Nicholas's Island, 30,
    31
Dungy Head, 159, 161
Dunscombe Cliff, 93–4
Durdle Door, 159, 160, 161
Durl Head, 73
Durlston, 183
Durlston Bay, 185
Durlston Castle, 184, 185
Durlston Country Park, 183, 185
Durlston Head, 181, 183, 189

East Budleigh, 86
East Cliff, Beer (National Trust),
    100
East Cliff, Bridport, 129, 130
East Ebb Cove, 126
East Fleet, 140, 141, 142, 143
East Man, 181, 182
East Portlemouth, 53
East Portlemouth Church, 53–4
East Prawle, 56
Eastwood, John, 124, 128
Ebenezer, 143, 218

Edward I, King, 117
Edward III, King, 80
Edward VII, King, 163
Egmont Bight, 177
Egmont Point, 177
Elberry Cove, 74
Eldon, Earl of, 177
Elizabeth I, Queen, 33, 117, 125
Emmett's Hill, 179, 181
Encombe, 177
Encombe House, 177
Enterprise Neptune Appeal, 121
Erme Mouth, 39, 40
Erme River, 41, 43, 54
Essex, Earl of, 30
Exe River, 79, 80, 81
Exeter, 79, 80
Exmoor, 80
Exmouth, 79, 80–2
Eype Village, 126
Eype's Mouth, 125, 126–7

Falkner, J. Meade, 142
Ferries, 223–6
Ferry Bridge, 143–4
Ferry Wood, 35
Field, John, 139
Fisher's Place, 153–4
Fleet, 139, 141, 143, 144, 202, 217, 218, 220, 221
Fleet House (Moonfleet Manor), 142
The Floors, 84
Flower's Barrow, 15, 170–1
Foreland (Handfast Point), 185, 187–8
Forestry Commission High Peak conifer plantation, 89
Fort Bovisand Underwater Centre, 31
Fort Charles, Salcombe Castle, 53
Fortescue, Sir Edmund, 53
Fortuneswell, 219

Fossil Forest, 165, 166
Foxhole Cove, 57
Franklin, Jane, 165
Frenchman's Rock, 57
Freshwater (near Bridport), 130, 132
Freshwater (near Egmont Bight), 177
Freshwater (near Westcombe Beach), 42
Froude, J.A., 50
Furzey Island, 194

Gad Cliff, 173
Gallants' Bower, 69
Gammon Head, 56
Gara Point, 35
Gara Rock, 55
Gara Rock Hotel, 55
Gaulter Gap, 174
George III, King, 148, 149–50, 169, 204, 210, 211, 218
Glebe Cottage, Ringstead, 153
Gold Down, 173
Golden Cap, 15, 117, 122–3, 124, 125, 201
Golden Cap Estate (National Trust), 121–2
Goodrington Sands, 75
Gore Cove, 142
Gould's Bottom, 204
Great Ebb, 126
Great Globe, Swanage, 183–5
Great Hill, 203, 204
Great Mattiscombe Sand, 57
Great Mew Stone, 31–2, 35
Great Seaside Farm, Branscombe, 99, 101
Green Hill Barton, 209
Green Island, 194
Grove Hill Bottom, 203
Gull Island, 57

Hallsands, 55, 57, 59–60
Hambury Tout, 159, 161
Hamoaze, 30
Ham Stone, 56
Ham Stone Cove, 56
Hamworthy, 194
Handfast Point (Foreland), 185, 187–8, 189, 191
Hardy, Thomas, 124, 150, 156, 207
Hardy Monument (Admiral Sir Thomas Hardy), 140, 200, 201, 202
Hartshorn Plantation, 62
Hawley, Sir John, 69, 70, 71
Hayes Barton, 85, 86
Hazel Tor, 48
Heath, Sidney, 59, 61, 152, 170
Heath Range, Lulworth, 164
Hedbury Quarry, 182
Hele, Sir John, 33
Hell Stone, 200–1
Hen Cliff, 175
Hengistbury Head, 188, 189
Henry VIII, King, 53, 117, 145
Herbury, 142, 220
Herzogin Cecilie, 48
Heybrook Bay, 31
High Land of Orcombe (National Trust), 82
Higher Dunscombe Cliff, 94
Hobarrow Bay, 173
Holbeton, 40–1
Holcombe, 78
Holcombe Vale, 170
Holworth, 155–6
Holworth Cliff, 155
Holy Trinity Church, Bincombe, 207
Hooken Cliffs, 100
Hope Cove, 47
Hope's Nose, 76
Hopkins, Edric, 50–1
Horsley Cove, 56

Houns-tout, 177
Hugo, Victor, 221

Inner Hope, 47
The Island (off Prawle Point), 56
Isle of Wight, 188, 191, 192

Jackman, Brian, 205
Jarvis, Richard of Rickham, 54
Jennycliff Bay, 30
Jesty, Benjamin, 182
Jordan Hill Roman temple, 151–2
Jordan river, 152

Keleway, John, 97
Kimmeridge, 173–5, 176, 179
Kimmeridge Bay, 173, 175, 176
Kimmeridge Coal (blackstone), 175
Kimmeridge Ledges, 176
Kingsbridge Estuary, 49
King's Head Rock, 57
Kingston, 177
Kingswear, 69, 71, 72
Kingswear Castle, 69, 70, 71
Knoll Plantation, 198–9

Labrador Bay, 76
Ladram Bay, 88–9
Landslip, 104–7
Lane, William, 42
Langerstone Point, 56
Langstone Rock, 79
Langton Herring, 141
Langton Hive Point, 220
Lannacombe, 57
Lawrence, Sergeant John, 189, 191
Lawrence's Cottage, 136
Legg, Rodney, 164, 175
Leland, Itinerary by, 84
Lim River, 117
Limekiln Hill, 198
Linton Hill, 140
Little Bindon, 165

Little Sea, 15
Littlecombe Shoot, 96, 97
Littleham Cove, 83, 84
Litton Cheney Youth Hostel, 135
Look Farm, 135
Louterell, Sir Geoffrey, 169
Lower Ley, 62
Lulworth, Lulworth Cove, 158,
    159, 161, 162–4, 165, 171, 209,
    211
Lulworth Camp, 167
Lulworth Castle, 167, 168, 169, 170
Lulworth Manor, 169
Lulworth Ranges (MOD), 164–5,
    166, 170, 227
Luttrell Psalter, 169
Lyme Regis, 105, 107–8, 117–20,
    123
    Cobb, 107, 117, 118
    Philpot Museum, 119
Lynch Cove, 143

Maceley Cove, 56
Maiden Castle, 204
Maiden Plantation, 169
Maidencombe, 76
Man Sands, 72
Mann, Thomas, 150
Manor House Farm, 135, 198
Martin, Sarah, 35
Martinstown, 203, 204
Mattiscombe/Matchcombe Beach,
    57
Mayflower, 30, 69
Melcombe Regis, 144, 148, 149,
    150, 153, 203, 209
Merry Hill, 140
Middle Bottom 159
Mill Bay, 54, 55
Mill Bay Cove, 71, 72
Millais, Sir John, 85–6
Milton Abbas, 155
Minehead, 13

Mohun, Eleanor (Lady Carew), 65
Monmouth, Duke of, 15, 118, 119
Moonfleet, 65
Morcombelake village, 121, 122
Mothecombe, 39
The Moult, Salcombe, 50
Mouthstone Point, 35
Mowat, Farley, 131
Mowlem, John, 185
Mupe Bay, 167
Mupe Rocks, 166

Narborough, Lady, 33
National Conservation Corps, 105
National Nature Reserves, 59,
    104–7, 191–2
National Parks and Access to the
    Countryside Act (1949), 13
National Trust, 33, 48, 49, 50–2,
    56, 69, 73, 82, 94, 97, 99, 100,
    120, 121, 131, 132, 154, 155,
    183, 187, 188, 191, 199
    addresses, 227
Needles, 188, 191
Nelson, Frances, Lady, 80
Ness Beach, 76–7
Netton Down, 37
New Barn Farm, 141
New Swanage, 187
Newcomen, Elias, 65
Newcomen, Thomas, 65, 71
Newcomen Society, 71
Newman, John, 207
Newton, 35
Newton Creek, 35
Newton Ferrers, 34, 35
Nodding Donkey oil well, 173, 175,
    176
No Man's Land, 188
Northdown Barn, 209
Northover, Peter, 128
Noss, 35
Noss Mayo, 34

Nunnery Grove, 140

Oddicombe funicular, 14, 76, 77
Old Harry Rocks, 188, 191
Old Harry's Wife, 188
Old Lyme Hill, 120
Old Nick's Ground, 188
Osmington, 14, 209, 210, 211–12
Osmington Forge, 211, 212
Osmington Holiday Club, 213
Osmington Mills, 152–3, 212, 213
Othona, 134
Otter Cover, 83
Otter River, 84, 86, 87–8, 89
Otterton, 84, 89
Otterton Edge, 87
Ottery St Mary, 84
Ottery Venn, 84
Outer Hope, 47
'Outrage' storm, Chesil (1824), 142, 217–18
Overbeck, Otto Ludwig, 51
Overcombe Corner, 151
Overmoigne, 156

Paignton, 75
Palmerston Forts, 30, 31
Parson's Barn, 188
Peak Hill, 90
Peartree Cove, 57
Peartree Point, 57
Pepler's Point, Lulworth, 163, 164
Peveril Point, 181, 185, 186
Pevsner, Nikolaus, 41, 207
Picklecombe Fort, 31
Pig's Nose headland, 56
Pilchard Cove, 63
Pilgrim Fathers, 30, 69
Pinnacles, 57
Pliosaurus grandis, 174
Plumleigh, Barbara, 70–1
Plym River, 30, 43
Plymouth, 29–30

Plymouth Breakwater, 31
Plymouth Sound, 29, 30
Poole, 149, 194
Poole Bay, 187, 188, 191
Poole Harbour, 192, 193
Poolness Beach, 88
Portesham, 200, 201
Portesham Hill, 200
Portland, 100, 108, 123, 131, 144, 145, 159, 200, 201, 202, 203, 205, 217, 221
Portland Bill, 117
Portland Harbour, 146, 209, 221
Portland Roads, 143
Port Light Hotel, 48
Poundhouse, 65
Poxwell, 209, 211
Prawle Point, 35, 56
Preston, 208, 209
Proust, Marcel, 150
Puncknowle, 135, 199
Purbeck Hills, 188
Purbeck House, Swanage, 186

Radar Crossroads, 167
Radipole, 148, 149
Railways, 227
Ralegh, Sir Walter, 29, 33, 71, 85, 86
Rattenbury, Jack, 103
Raven's Cove, 57
Redcliff Point, 152
Redend Point, 191
Renscombe Farm, 179
Revelstoke, St Peter's Church, 37–8
Richards, Rev. John, 175–6
Rickham Common, 54
Ridge Barn, 121
Ridge Bottom, 203
Ridge Cliff, 125
Ridge Water, 121
Ringmore, 42–3
Ring's Hill, 170

Ringstead, 153–4
Ringstead Bay (National Trust),
    154, 155
Rock End Path, 76
Roope, John, 71
Rope Lake Point, 176
Rousdon, 106
Rudder Cove, 55

St Aldhelm's Chapel, 179–80
St Aldhelm's Head, 179–81
St Aldhelm's Point, 176
St Anchorite's Rock, 39, 41
St Andrew's Church, Lulworth, 169
St Andrew's Church, Lyme Regis,
    120
St Catherine by the Sea, Holworth,
    155–6
St Catherine's Chapel, Abbotsbury,
    138, 139, 140, 218
St Gabriel's Church, 121
St Gregory's Church, Seaton,
    102–4
St James's Church, Kingston, 177
St James's Church, Slapton, 63
St Lucas Leap, 188
St Mary's Bay, 73
St Mary's Church, Lulworth Castle,
    168, 169
St Nicholas of Myra, Studland,
    189–90
St Nicholas of Myra, Worth
    Matravers, 182
St Osmund's Church, Osmington,
    211
St Oswald's Bay, 159, 161
St Peter the Poor Fisherman,
    Revelstoke, 37–8
St Petroc's Church, Dartmouth, 70
St Saviour's Church, Darmouth, 71
St Werburgh, 32–3
St Winwaloe of Portlemouth, 53, 54
Salcombe, 50–3

Salcombe Castle (Fort Charles), 53
Salcombe Estuary, 48, 51
Salcombe Harbour, 43, 50
Sandsfoot Castle, 145–6
Sandy Bay, 82–3
Sandy Causeway, 42
Scabbacombe Lane, 72
Scratchy Bottom, 159, 160
Sea Barn Farm, 156
Seacombe, 182
Seacombe Bottom, 182
Seacombe Sand, 55
Seaton, 101–4, 105
    St Gregory's Church, 102–3
    tramway, 102, 103
Seaton Bay, 106
Seaton Hole, 101
Seatown, 123–4
Sequers Bridge, 40
Shaldon, 76–7, 78
Sharkham Point, 73
Sharp Tor, 50
Sharpitor House (National Trust),
    50–2
Shell Bay, 191, 192, 193
Sherriff, R.C., 42
Shiglehill Cove, 66
Shortlake House, 152
Sid River, 91, 92
Sidmouth, 90–2, 93, 101
Skerries Bank, 58
Slapton Ley, 15, 61–2, 63
Slapton Ley Field Study Centre, 62,
    63
Slapton Sands, 61, 62, 63
Slapton village, 62, 63
The Slide, 63
Small Mouth, 144, 218, 221
Small's Cove, 54
Smeaton's Lighthouse, Plymouth,
    30
Smugglers' Cave, 166
Snellings Down, 37

Soar Mill Cove, 48, 49
Southcombe Farm, 93
Southdown Cliff, 72
Southdown National Trust, 73
South Farm, 86, 87
South Gwyle, 177
South Hams, 42–3, 62
South Haven Point, 13, 192
South Milton Ley, 46
South West Way Association, 13,
    59, 64, 86, 181, 197
South Winterbourne, 204
The Spittle, 120
Soring Bottom, 208, 209
Staddon Fort, 31
Staddon Heights, 31
Stair Hole, Lulworth, 162, 163
Stamford Fort, Plymouth, 30
Stanton St Gabriel, 122
Starcross, 78, 79–80
Starehole Bay, 50
Starehole Cove, 48
Starre, John, 103–4
Start, 57–8
Start Bay, 58, 59
Start Bay Youth Hostel, 63–4
Start Farm, 59
Start Point, 58, 100, 123, 198
Stinking Cove, 57
Stoke Fleming, 61, 64, 65
Stoke Fleming Church, 64–5
Stoke House, 37
Stoke Point, 37
Stonebarrow Hill, 121
Stonehouse, 29
Straight Point, 82
Strangeways, Sir Giles, 139
Strete, 64
Strete Church, 63
Studland, 187, 189–91, 192
Studland Bay, 15, 187, 189, 192
Studland Beach, 191
Studland Hill (National Trust), 187

Studland Wood, 189
Sudstone (Sutton), 29
Sugary Cove, 69
Sutton Poyntz, 208, 209
Swanage, 181, 185–7, 193
    The Great Globe, 183–5
Swanage Bay, 185, 187
Swyre, 135
Swyre Head, 158, 159, 160, 177

Tallis Rock Hotel, 64
Tamar River, 30
Teign River, 78
Teignmouth, 76, 77, 78
Tennyson, Alfred, Lord, 50, 119
Thorncombe Beacon, 125, 126
Thurlestone, 45, 46
Thurlestone Golf Course, 45–6
Tidmoor Point, 143
Tilly Whim Caves, 183
Timber Hill, 120
Tinsey Head, 60
Top of Bincleaves, 146
Torbay, 76
Torbay and Dartmouth Steam
    Line, 14, 75
Torcross, 60, 61
Torcross Point, 60, 61
Tourist Boards, 228
Tregarthin, Joan, 97–8
Treves, Frederick, 163–4, 177, 185
Tulk's Hill, 199
Turnchapel, 30
Twopenny Loaf Rock, 88
Tyneham, 171–3
Tyneham Gap, 173
Tyneham Gwyle, 171

Ulwell Road, Swanage, 187
Undercliff (Underbarn) Walk, 146
Under Freestone, 182
Upcot Farm, 121
Upwey, 204

Vain Farm, 199
Vereker, G.M., 51
Victoria, Queen, 92, 150

Wadham, John, 97–8
Wagon Rock, 173
Wakeham, Samuel, 32
Wareham, 187
Warham family, 211
The Warren, Devon, 35
The Warren, Dorset, 159
Warren Cottage, 35, 37
Warren Cove, 65
Warren Point, 34, 35
Warren Wood, 189
Watcombe Head, 76
Wear Cliff, 123
Wear's Hill, 199–200
Weld, Cardinal, 169
Weld family, 169
Weld, Thomas, 125, 169, 170
Wembury, 32, 33, 35
Wembury Beach, 32
Wembury Parish Church, 32–3
Wembury Point, 31
West Allington, 126
West Bay, 126, 127–9, 217, 219
West Bexington, 14, 135, 136, 198
West Bottom, 159
West Cliff, Bridport, 127, 128
West Down Beacon, 84
West Elworth, 140
West Fleet, 141
West Hill, 209
West Lulworth, 165
West Man, 181
Westacott, Hugh, 39, 58
Westcombe Beach, 42
Westhay, 121, 122
Westhay Water, 121
Weston Cliff, 95
Weston Mouth, 94–5, 97

Wey River, 148
Weymouth, 129, 143–51, 175, 197,
    203, 204
  Harbour, 146, 148, 149
  King's Statue, 150, 151
  Nothe Fort and Gardens, 147
  Sandsfoot Castle, 145–6
Weymouth Bay, 159
Whitcombe, 209
White, R.C., 157
White Cliff, 101
White Hill, 200
White Horse Hill, 209, 210, 211
White Nothe, 154, 156–7, 158
Whiteway Hill, 171
Widdicombe Ley, 60
Wightman, Ralph, 117, 123
Willow Cove, 66
Willy, Margaret, 52
Windgate, 90
Windward Cottage, 65
Winfrith Atomic Energy
    Establishment, 15, 170
Winspit, 180
Winspit Bottom, 181
Winterbourne St Martin, 203
Wonwell Beach, 41
Woolbrook Cottage (now Royal
    Glen Hotel), Sidmouth, 92
Worbarrow, 171, 173
Worbarrow Bay, 171
Worbarrow Tout, 171
Worth Matravers, 179, 182
Wyke Regis, 221
Wyke Wood, 141
Wynreford River, 124

Yealm Mouth, 36
Yealm River, 34, 43
Yealmpton, 34–5
Youth Hostels, 228–9